Praise for *Who Do You Serve,*

"This brilliant collection of essa s,
community organizers and survivors of state violence, urgently confronts the criminalization, police violence and anti-Black racism that
is plaguing urban communities. It is one of the most important books
to emerge about these critical issues: passionately written, with a keen
eye toward building a world free of the cruelty and violence of the
carceral state."
**–Beth Richie, author of "Arrested Justice: Black Women,
Violence, and America's Prison Nation"**

"'Who Do You Serve, Who Do You Protect?' is a powerful collection
of essays by organizers, legal activists and progressive journalists that
takes us beyond the 'few bad apples' theory of police violence, insisting
that we interrogate the essential role and purpose of police and policing in our society. These writers have highlighted some of the critical
questions that the anti-state-violence movement is wrestling with."
**–Barbara Ransby, author of "Ella Baker and the Black Freedom
Movement: A Radical Democratic Vision"**

"This timely and essential set of essays written by activists, organizers
and journalists offers a window into our particular historical moment
centered on an ongoing struggle against state violence. As a longtime organizer immersed in the current Movement for Black Lives,
I read the contributions hoping to learn and to be inspired. I found
the essays to be informative, illuminating and challenging. The book
covers topics ranging from police torture and the fight for accountability to how we might best engage in transformative organizing
that could lead to a world without police. I cannot recommend this
anthology any more highly. It's an indispensable primer for anyone
who wants to understand the current rebellions and uprisings against
police impunity."
–Mariame Kaba, founder and director of Project NIA

"'Who Do You Serve, Who Do You Protect?' is an extraordinary collection of writings by activists living and working at the epicenter of police violence and the anti-Blackness and structural racism so foundational to US systems of policing. Simultaneously enraging, invigorating, radically imaginative, practical and inspiring, this essential book relocates justice in accountable social, economic and cultural relationships, pointing the way toward foundational transformation rather than cosmetic reform."

–Kay Whitlock, co-author of "Considering Hate"
and "Queer (In)Justice"

"America is at war, and the violence that propels that war is largely directed at people of color, especially Black youth. One instance of such a war is evident in the violence by the police against Black communities, the criminalization of everyday behavior, the assaults on Black bodies, and the ever-growing incarceration state. 'Who Do You Serve, Who Do You Protect?' addresses this violence in a way no other book has done in the last forty years. It reveals the underlying causes, economic and ideological, that drive such violence so as to provide a comprehensive understanding of its roots, its multiple layers, history, and different forms, while at the same time it offers a discourse of critical engagement and transformation in order to address it. 'Who Do You Serve, Who Do You Protect?' is an invaluable resource for asking questions about the emergence of racist violence and state terrorism as a defining principle of everyday life and how they can be addressed. Everyone who cares about justice and democracy and a future in which they mutually inform each other should read this book."

–Henry Giroux, author of "Disposable Futures:
The Seduction of Violence in the Age of Spectacle"

"We know the names: Trayvon Martin, Michael Brown, Freddie Gray, Eric Garner, Sandra Bland, Tamir Rice, Rekia Boyd, Laquan McDonald. And we've seen the uprisings: L.A., Ferguson, Baltimore, Chicago. "Who Do You Serve, Who Do You Protect?" goes behind the headlines to ask the deeper questions: Do the police make communities (particularly, communities where Black and Brown people live) safer? Who do community residents fear? Are there ways to ad-

dress those fears without the police and carceral state? What would we have to create in order to do this? What steps must we take to get there? Each of the essays examines these interrelated questions in depth. Read together, they provide an extremely thorough, and timely, examination of the issues underlying these recent events, forcing us to rethink the very idea of justice in this country."
—Alan Mills, Uptown People's Law Center

"Resisting state-sanctioned violence, especially by police, has become a paramount issue as a result of grassroots activists mobilizing throughout the country. 'Who Do You Serve, Who Do You Protect?' gives journalists, writers, and activists at the forefront of activism and reporting on state-sanctioned violence in the United States a welcome platform to present their ideas for growing a movement against this violence so activists may have a lasting impact, which empowers and lifts up communities of color."
—Kevin Gosztola, managing editor of Shadowproof.com

WHO DO YOU SERVE, WHO DO YOU PROTECT?

Police Violence and Resistance in the United States

Edited by Maya Schenwar, Joe Macaré and Alana Yu-lan Price
Foreword by Alicia Garza

Haymarket Books
Chicago, Illinois

To everyone engaged in the struggle against police violence in the United States and beyond.

Published in 2016 by
Haymarket Books
P.O. Box 180165
Chicago, IL 60618
773-583-7884
www.haymarketbooks.org
info@haymarketbooks.org

ISBN: 978-1-60846-612-2

Distributed to the trade in the US through Consortium Book Sales
and Distribution (www.cbsd.com) and internationally through
Ingram Publisher Services International (www.ingramcontent.com).

This book was published with the generous support of Lannan
Foundation and Wallace Action Fund.

Special discounts are available for bulk purchases by organizations
and institutions. Please call 773-583-7884 or email
info@haymarketbooks.org for more information.

Cover design by Rachel Cohen. Cover art by Jared Rodriguez.

Printed in the United States.

Library of Congress Cataloging-in-Publication data is available.

CONTENTS

Foreword

Alicia Garza

Black people are fighting for our right to live while Black.

2010 marked the beginning of a historic period of Black resistance to police terrorism and state-sanctioned violence. Beginning with the murder of Oscar Grant in January 2010 by then-BART police officer Johannes Mehserle, and continuing with the high-profile cases of Trayvon Martin, Jordan Davis, Renisha McBride, Michael Brown, Rekia Boyd, Tamir Rice and too many others, police violence, particularly in poor and Black communities, has taken center stage nationwide.

The rebellion that ensued in August 2014 after the death of Michael Brown in Ferguson, Missouri, was for some a politicizing moment, the defining moment that spurred them into social justice activism and/or organizing. For others, it was yet another moment to advance a demand that has been emanating from our communities since Black people first reached the shores of America—a demand to stop the physical, emotional, economic and political slaughter of Black bodies.

Police violence is not a new phenomenon in Black communities. Modern-day policing locates its origins in the slave economy, which helped build the wealth and the industrialized economy of this nation and of other nations around the world. Policing in the context of slavery was intended to ensure the protection of private property owners—with the private property being Black human beings.[1]

After slavery was "legally" abolished in 1865 with the passage of the 13th Amendment, policing adapted itself to maintain white supremacy through the use of force and racial terror by making slavery and indentured servitude illegal—except for anyone convicted of a crime. The so-called emancipation of Black people from slavery transformed physical bondage into systems of economic, political and social disenfranchisement. The criminalization of Black people and Blackness, reflected in the prison-industrial complex, is an extension of slavery and the slave economy.

Sharecropping, Jim Crow segregation, and other forms of exclusion and exploitation that kept (and keep) Black people from accessing social, economic or political power have been rigorously enforced and maintained with the assistance of police departments. Beginning in the 1930s and throughout the height of the civil rights movement in the 1950s and 1960s, it was commonplace for a local sheriff, the head of the Chamber of Commerce, or the local mayor to attend an evening meeting of the Ku Klux Klan—not necessarily because they hated Black people (though some certainly did), but mostly because they feared the loss of white power over Black human beings and our potential.

In the above context, police violence was used to reinforce and maintain an economic structure that preys on Black bodies, where those who "owned" the most Black bodies secured the political power needed to control the furtherance of such an arrangement. It continues to be so used. There are now more of us grappling with the contradiction of how to keep our communities safe when those who are entrusted with our protection and safety are rarely (if ever) charged when they themselves are the purveyors of harm.

The rise of prisons as a booming industry has led to entire local economies that are dependent upon police, policing, punishment and retribution, largely against Black bodies—whether they be cisgender or transgender, gay or straight, of men or of women. Furthermore, the security and surveillance industries provide economic security for a group of people that has largely been dislocated from the formal economy. At the same time, those industries target Black people, interrupt Black families, and continue to further the notion that Black people are to be punished and watched, and are certainly not to be trusted.

Inside those cages where we have disappeared more than 1 million Black bodies, many are forced to work for corporations like Kmart and J. C. Penney, who subcontract with the state to manufacture jeans inside the walls of prisons. Others are forced to provide critical public services like fighting fires for less than a dollar a day.[2] The capture of Black bodies to be bought or sold has always been a big business in the United States, and while there may no longer be an overseer with a lash, there is now a deputy with a gun.

Criminalization and police violence do not just impact Black communities, though Black communities are disproportionately affected given our relative population. Latinos and First Nations people are also severely affected by policing that preys predominantly on poor bodies of color.

When Patrisse Cullors, Opal Tometi and I started #BlackLivesMatter—an organizing network fighting back against anti-Black racism and state-sanctioned violence—in 2013, after George Zimmerman was acquitted in the murder of teenager Trayvon Martin, we understood that what's happening to Black people in this country and around the world is much larger than just police and policing alone. Poverty, unemployment, lack of access to quality and affordable education, and HIV/AIDS are just a few of the issues impacting Black people disproportionately to our percentage of the population.

When Zimmerman murdered an unarmed Black child and got away with it, we saw not just an individual act of cowardice and prejudice expressed as vigilantism, but also the effects of a highly racist society that sees Black bodies as disposable. Even Zimmerman's defense—claiming he was scared for his life and forced to act in "self-defense"—reflects the deeply ingrained fear of Black bodies, particularly Black male bodies, in a society shaped by the largely racist war on drugs, which demonizes Black men and portrays them as a potential threat that must be eliminated.

Of course, police violence and state-sanctioned violence do not just impact cisgender Black men. Black women like Rekia Boyd, Renisha McBride and Mya Hall are also caught in this web. Roughly 35 percent of Black trans folks have been arrested or held in a cell due to bias at some point in their lives, and more than half of Black trans folks report discomfort seeking police assistance, according to the National LGBTQ Task Force.

Just last year, a police officer was arrested for allegedly sexually assaulting Black women during traffic stops in Oklahoma City, Oklahoma. In fact, Black women are more likely to be sexually assaulted by the police than we are to be killed by them. Yet police kill us too: Natasha McKenna and Sandra Bland were killed while in police custody, and questions still remain after their deaths.

Black people are being disappeared at the rate of one every 28 hours by police or vigilante violence, yet those who are taking their lives are rarely (if ever) held accountable.[3]

Many living in America might never have thought to question the need for police—and in particular this style of punitive policing—were it not for the social uprisings that have taken place over the last five years (most notably the last year and a half).

What can and will be done to hold police accountable for the violence that they enact in our communities? What happens when we question the fundamental assumption that police and policing are our only option for community safety? These questions are far from theoretical. A vision for a new world in which police and policing are replaced with new ways of keeping each other safe and holding each other accountable is already brewing. The articles in this collection are meant to further this crucial discussion, describing the challenges that we face in a society that is increasingly over-policed and offering provocative ideas for what a new world might look like.

Introduction

Maya Schenwar, Joe Macaré and Alana Yu-lan Price

"To Protect and Serve" won the Los Angeles Police Department's motto contest in 1955, and in the decades since, the slogan has been slapped on patrol cars across the country.[1] Though it's catchy, the motto is remarkably unspecific: Who—or what—is being protected? Who is being served? What are police actually doing in the United States, and toward what ends?

At Truthout we've consistently endeavored to address these questions through a journalistic lens. Historically, the most harmful impacts of policing have often been kept from the news headlines. In fact, journalism's systematic failure to report on police violence has fueled the continuation of this violence. However, since the murder of Mike Brown, we've seen a surge in media attention to anti-Black police violence. In this climate of heightened media awareness, Truthout has continued its longstanding attention to these issues. Instead of simply reporting on current instances of violence and compiling shocking statistics, we've striven to draw a more comprehensive picture of policing in the context of American racism—particularly anti-Black racism—and oppression. The question, for us, is not "How do we confront the fact that police are doing things that are wrong?" but rather "How do we confront the institution of policing as a whole—an institution whose entire grounding and current practice is wrong?"

1

To confront this question, we must focus in on how recent police killings of young people of color in the US fit into the historical and global contexts of anti-Black racism, as well as racism and xenophobia more broadly. In this collection, we've pulled together essays from a wide range of Truthout contributors, probing at questions about the purpose of the police and what they accomplish in the United States. In addition to focusing on anti-Black violence, this book explores police violence against Brown, Indigenous and other marginalized communities, drawing connections between these overlapping manifestations of oppression.

Influenced by the work of Mariame Kaba, Beth Richie, Michelle Alexander, Angela Y. Davis, Fania Davis, Che and Reina Gossett, Dean Spade, Ruthie Wilson Gilmore and Mimi Kim, and inspired by the work of restorative and transformative justice activists across the country, we have drawn together articles that not only expose the racism and violence of policing in the United States but also report on efforts to develop alternative methods to keep each other safe.

The past couple of years have been a time of mass action, movement building and collective struggle. The pieces in the latter part of this collection delve into these movements and their long-term meanings, exploring what is being struggled against and what is being built. The second half of this book also asks: If not the police, then what? We can't fully challenge the institution of the police without discussing alternative ways of fostering safety in our communities.

Policing, Racist Violence and False Notions of Safety

The book's first essay, "Killing the Future: The Theft of Black Life" by Nicholas Powers, tackles the significance of anti-Black police violence head-on, examining how Black children "aren't seen as part of the future" and are deemed "disposable" by both the police that bully them and the society that incarcerates them en masse. In Chapter 2, an investigation into police coercion and framing in Detroit, Aaron Cantú demonstrates how police orchestrated false murder convictions for a number of Black men using jailhouse informants—convictions that resulted in decades-long and sometimes lifelong prison sentences. One of these men is now fighting to be released—and that fight has revealed a deep-seated culture of racist, systemic corruption.

Of course, police corruption is not confined to one city or one department. In their investigative report in Chapter 3, Sarah Macaraeg and Alison Flowers uncover the failure of the City of Chicago to acknowledge the continued presence of repeat perpetrators of violence on its police force. The city's almost universal failure to fire or otherwise hold accountable officers who kill people—some officers have even been granted awards for it—is not unique or anachronistic; it ties in with a larger culture of white-supremacy-based policing, in which brutal violence against people of color is simply considered part of the job.

Also zeroing in on an example of larger structural dynamics drawn from Chicago, Adam Hudson traces the historical roots of police torture in the United States in "Beyond Homan Square" (Chapter 4). Hudson points out that whenever it becomes known that the US is perpetrating torture—whether in CIA black sites abroad or in police torture sites at home, such as Chicago's Homan Square—these instances are framed as anomalies. They are not anomalies; Hudson locates them within a long tradition of institutionalized torture, a practice embedded in the slavery, imperialism and colonialism on which the US was constructed.

On a similarly historical note, in Chapter 5, Roberto Rodriguez examines the "many tentacles" of violence against communities of color, including the deportation of large numbers of Latino migrants and the rarely publicized killings of undocumented and Indigenous people. He traces these intertwined strains of violence back to the era of colonialism and its racialized hierarchies, noting, "There has never been a time in the history of this country in which people of color were treated by the legal system as full human beings with corresponding full human rights."

In "Killing Africa" (Chapter 6), William C. Anderson notes that the struggles of Black people against police repression and violence are hardly specific to the United States: "In many different ways," he writes, "much of the world is invested in killing Africa." To combat this global web of violence, Anderson calls for an international movement that centers the needs of the African diaspora, addressing not only policing but also colonialism, imperialism and economic violence.

In addition to being deeply racialized, policing and police violence are deeply gendered. Looking at the stories of Sandra Bland, Mya Hall, Janisha Fonville and others, Andrea J. Ritchie examines the patterns of police violence against women and trans and queer people of color in Chapter 7. Ritchie rightly insists that we must center the experiences of women and trans people of color in conversations around police violence—as well as in discussions of how to move toward a radical reimagining of public safety.

Gendered police violence also plays out in the acts for which people are criminalized. In Chapter 8, Victoria Law reports on the vulnerability that pregnant people face in their encounters with police, exposing police encroachment into the lives of pregnant people of color and other marginalized groups. Of course, policing weighs heavily not only on pregnancies but also on parenting. Eisa Nefertari Ulen's essay "Black Parenting Matters" (Chapter 9) explores the terror and sadness that many Black parents experience in the face of the realization that their children may face racist policing, and dreams of liberation for her own son.

A Police-Free Future?

What does "being free" mean, in relation to the police? Rachel Herzing has an answer: Instead of "police reform"—slapping Band-Aids on torture and death—we must find ways to shrink the role of police in our lives, striving toward the eventual abolition of the institution of police. In Chapter 10, Herzing lights the way down that path.

The role of youth has been central in the current struggle against racist police violence. The Chicago-based group We Charge Genocide, founded and led primarily by Black youth, made its way to the United Nations to present testimony on the killing of young Black people by Chicago police. Asha Rosa, Monica Trinidad and Page

May chronicle the group's journey in "We Charge Genocide: The Emergence of a Movement" (Chapter 11).

Not only are Black women some of the primary targets of police violence, they are also at the forefront of the struggle against it, as Thandi Chimurenga describes in Chapter 12. In fact, it was three Black queer women who originated the #BlackLivesMatter hashtag and led its transformation into a movement.

Indigenous people are killed at a higher rate by police than any other racial group, and the role of Native activists in the movement for Black lives has underscored the intersection of Native and Black struggles against rampant state violence. In Chapter 13, Kelly Hayes highlights the groups' intersecting oppressions—and also acknowledges the rifts that have built up over the centuries between Black and Native communities, as each has struggled against multiple types of state violence. Nevertheless, Hayes writes, "Many of us believe that neither of our communities can be free without the liberation of the other."

In Chapter 14 Mike Ludwig urges readers to consider making an unusual New Year's resolution: "Don't Call the Police." Ludwig isn't saying that those who do call the police are somehow betraying their communities; rather, he holds that resolving to avoid unnecessary 911 calls is simultaneously a protest against a racist and brutal system and a challenge to create vibrant new structures with which to build safety.

What would a world beyond policing look like? In Chapter 15, Candice Bernd profiles community groups that are working to provide "first-response" care in ways that minimize contact with the police, particularly in the case of mental health emergencies and other situations in which police have a proven record of exacerbating the immediate circumstances of those involved. These experiments—grounded in the principle of neighbors caring for neighbors—provide glimmers of how we might create our own modes of safety and security.

This book ends with "Building Community Safety: Practical Steps Toward Liberatory Transformation," in which Ejeris Dixon takes on the question often avoided by even the most adamant opponents of policing: How do we confront violence, if not by deploying armed

state forces to fight it? Dixon, drawing from her own community organizing experience, instructs us to build alternative forms of community safety with as much energy as we fight police violence, even when
the fruits of our organizing aren't immediately, vividly apparent.

Challenging the police as an institution must involve asking big
and unsettling questions. What does being safe even mean? How
many of our society's assumptions about safety are grounded in racism, injustice and violence? If we can't count on an ever-present state
"service" to "protect" us, what can we count on?

Is it possible to build toward a world in which we can count on
each other?

PART I: POLICE FAILING TO SERVE AND PROTECT

1.

Killing the Future: The Theft of Black Life[1]

Nicholas Powers

"Tell me of the night your son was killed by the police," I asked. She sat up, and a deep sorrow moved in her eyes. "I had a habit of looking out the window to see my son," Danette Chavis said. "But that night, I said to myself, 'Oh, leave the boy alone,' and took a nap. The phone woke me up, and my daughter was rushing out of the door. I followed her and saw police tape, cops standing around a body. I yelled to see if it was him. But they wouldn't let me close. Later, I went to the morgue and identified my son."

We sat in the café; a few seconds passed in silence. She looked away as if seeing him dead for the first time, and I regretted asking the question. Around us, people typed on laptops or chatted over coffee. They were so carefree. How do we reach a city that mostly looks at people of color in contempt or pity rather than solidarity? How do we get them to listen?

I looked up from my notebook. "Ms. Chavis," I asked. "What do you miss most about your son?"

Making Wounds Speak

Imagine hearing that someone you love has died. Your heart would jump in your chest. Your body would clench like a fist around their memory. How angry would you be? How loud would you yell at the sky, at God, at anyone you could blame? Afterward, you'd float in a limbo of grief until you got answers, made sense of it and then slowly said goodbye. Gathering together with others at the funeral, you could complete the storyline of loss.

The stages of grief depend on narrative closure, the shoveling of dirt on the casket, the eulogizing of the dead. But for African-American parents whose children were slain by law enforcement, the stages of grief grind to a halt. The dead cannot be laid to rest because the cop who murdered them is not held accountable, and the violence is condoned. To eclipse the officer's guilt, the victims are "niggerized" in public. Have a criminal record? It will be paraded in public. Ever took silly gangsta photos? They will be proof of a "thug life." The parents see their child's image warped as they learn of more Black and Latino youth killed by cops. In a solidarity of despair, they embrace everyone's lost children, as if they can hear the dead repeating their final words, asking for their lives back.

In December 2014, 10 mothers whose children were killed by police held a rally in front of the US Department of Justice. Chavis was there and said into the megaphone, "None of us are safe. Law enforcement around the United States is brutalizing, arresting and murdering." A large group surrounded her with signs and candles. One by one the mothers spoke. Some had fought for years, like Chavis, who started a petition—now 35,000 signatures strong—to send to former Attorney General Eric Holder, or like Valerie Bell, whose son Sean was shot dead by New York City Police Department (NYPD) officers in 2006. Other grieving parents were more recently bereaved, like Jeralynn Blueford, whose son Alan was gunned down by Oakland police in 2012. She stood in front of the rally, choking on tears, saying, "Alan's last words were, 'Why did you shoot me?'"

Holding up the faces of their dead in front of the Department of Justice, the mothers confronted our nation's deepest contradiction. How can citizens be killed by agents of the very state that represents them, and no one be held accountable? All of them were women of color. Many were working-class. Their presence was already the answer. Beneath our formal trappings of democracy lies a long history of legal, race-based slavery and segregation, followed by a now-informal white supremacist regime in which white lives matter while Black ones don't.

The mothers rallied in front of the Department of Justice, but it was dark and empty. Faced with a closed building but wanting justice, they poured into the street and marched on Pennsylvania Avenue. Blocking traffic, they walked in between cars and shouted, "Shut it down! Shut it down!"

From Slave Chains to Handcuffs

Years ago, I visited a traveling exhibit on slavery and saw tourists standing quietly around a table filled with rusted shackles and chains. The host pointed at one and said it was worn by those enslaved in the Middle Passage. I reached out, fingertips hovering above it, then pulled back. "Go ahead," he said. "Touch it."

I lifted it and felt a heavy sadness rolling down my arms into the shackle. Slipping my hand inside, I thought of those in my family's past who were brought to this world wearing a thing like this. I wanted to rip the fucking metal apart. But I was only able to stand and hold a history I could not destroy.

Stealing Black lives at gunpoint is the most visible and violent evidence of history repeating in the present. To be Black in America is to be evidence of a theft. It is to be a descendant of human beings stolen from villages, stolen from their bodies, stolen from each other, sold and sold again. It is to see, in one's family history, ancestors stolen from their language, stolen from their land and left as walking targets. Inevitably we, their descendants, are shot at with everything from microaggressions to all-out physical violence, from suspicious stares to racial slurs, from stop-and-frisk to bullets.

To be Black in America is to know white supremacy is a culture of theft. We feel it like a tornado that one can try to sidestep but that sometimes descends on us anyway, ripping us out of our bodies. It's like an ancient vortex that split from another vortex, a slavery split from older forms of slavery that mixed with European capitalism, colonization and scientific racism. A whiteness took shape that churned through centuries and over continents, pulling people from their homes and "blackening" them. Whiteness is a social structure of extraction that rose in the triangular trade of slave ships, auction blocks and plantations. It was broken by the Civil War, remade as Jim Crow in segregated public spaces and redlined ghettos, then reinvented again as a war on drugs.

A few weeks ago, I reread Dr. Alexander Falconbridge's "An Account of the Slave Trade in the West Coast of Africa"; he was an 18th-century abolitionist who sailed on four slave ships. The descriptions were ghastly. "The men Negroes, on being brought aboard the ship, are immediately fastened together, two and two, by handcuffs on their wrists and by irons riveted on their legs," he wrote. "They are frequently stowed so close, as to admit of no other position than lying on their sides."

At home, I put down the book and picked up an autobiography written by one of my students at the state college where I work. Every year I teach a class in which students write 30-page memoirs, and many talk of family members in jail. This semester, one wrote of visiting her father in prison. At times, she was sad he was gone. Other times, she was angry and punished him by not visiting. But eventually she came back to see him. Year after year passed; he aged into a gray, bitter man, helplessly enraged that he missed out on her life. She wrote of leaving the prison and seeing men shuffling in leg chains; I couldn't help but think of Falconbridge's image of Black men with "irons riveted on their legs."

The Thin Blue Line

"Is it not enough that we are torn from our country and friends to toil for your luxury and lust of gain? Must every tender feeling be likewise sacrificed to your avarice?" wrote freed slave Olaudah Equiano in 1794, in his narrative of the Atlantic slave trade. "Why are parents to lose their children, brothers, sisters, or husbands their wives?"

The conflict that has driven history in the New World is Black people's struggle to hold onto their humanity against a culture that objectifies them as property. Twelve million Africans were sold across the Americas. Wherever they landed, they fought back, and when they did, white men representing the state attacked them. In Haiti, these white men wore French uniforms and shot muskets at rebels. In America, they were slave patrols, searching forests for runaways. Championed as heroes in their time, they killed with a clear conscience, because they saw us as semihumans who would wreck civilization if let loose. Blinded by whiteness, they were caught in a vast cultural superstructure that rose from the economic base of slavery. It gave them racial privileges in lieu of class ones; it taught them a visual vocabulary of darkies, Uncle Toms, niggers, mammies, jezebels and brutes. The blood they spilled from Black bodies was the implicit ink of America's social contract.

"Every drop of blood drawn with the lash shall be paid by another drawn with the sword," President Abraham Lincoln said in his second inaugural address. As smoke from the Civil War cleared, he pointed to the line we had crossed. Slavery was a national sin; those freed from it were its victims; those who defended it, the new villains. But it was a line trampled by white mobs and terrorist groups like the Ku Klux Klan, riding horses into the night to burn Black homes and then Black people themselves. The legal infrastructure of slavery was broken, but the culture of racism washed over the 13th, 14th and 15th Amendments like a tide, its deep currents pushing back against the new citizens. In order to survive, each generation of Black people picked up that line drawn between slavery and freedom, held it up and carried it forward. But at every step they took, they hit the thin blue wall of the police.

In the South, white plantation owners pushed for the Black Codes, which criminalized everyday life: being unemployed or failing to pay a tax became a crime. Cops pulled thousands of Black people into the ever-growing convict-lease system that recycled the debris of slavery into a new form. In the first wave of the Great Migration, nearly 2 million Black people fled the South to the cities of the

West, Midwest and Northeast. After their arrival, race riots blew up as white mobs hanged and shot Black people, and burned down Black neighborhoods. Police did not stop the violence.

Decades later, when Black people marched for civil rights in places like Selma, police beat them bloody. In the 1970s, when Black people defended themselves in groups like the Black Panthers, the police shot them down, leaving shattered windows and blood-soaked beds. In the 1980s and 1990s, when Black youth sold drugs to buy their way out of the ghetto, police killed or jailed a whole generation. And today, when Black and Latino youth want to walk freely, they are stopped and frisked by police.

In each generation, law enforcement has been the thin blue line against the Black freedom movement. Today the war on drugs, like the convict-lease system before it, has become an industry where the raw material fueling an ever-growing prison infrastructure is the criminalized Black body. From the economic base of mass incarceration a superstructure rises that trains white people, once again, to see "blackness" in a new version of the same old visual vocabulary—the drug dealer, the thug, the rapper, the hoe, the pimp and the junkie.

The old racial line between "Black" and "white" has been redrawn as the line between criminal and citizen. Up and down the class hierarchy from poor to wealthy, Black people have to dodge violence, from microaggressions to economic sabotage and from public shaming to physical attacks.

But always, it's the bullets that are the easiest to see. Most of us aren't killed by cops. Most of us "survive" racism. But every day another person of color is shot by police, and the holes left inside families are where loved ones used to breathe. The cops not only steal the lives of our children; they steal the lives of everyone who loved them. A part of us freezes in place, goes numb.

In the endless wait for justice, families carry memories that grow in the imagination. When I looked at Chavis' Facebook page, I saw a post about how her son Gregory would have been 29 this year. Other parents also keep track of the rites of passage their child should have had—like a wedding or graduation. The dead haunt us. They burn in our dreams. They ask for their time back. And more and more keep getting added to the roster of names, those shot down as the police aim at that invisible target on Black people, as they protect that line that so many pretend not to see.

To Protect and Serve

On March 1, 2015, four cops in Los Angeles' Skid Row wrestled a homeless Black man down on the ground. They looked like a giant squid, wrapped around him as he thrashed in their grip. A lone gunshot echoed. Then a loud volley of gunfire as his body fell silent. In the seconds afterward, they backed up as an angry crowd gathered and one man shouted, "Motherfucker! Motherfucker! They just killed that man!"

As I write this in the early months of 2015, more than 300 people have been murdered by police, only a tiny fraction of them in a gunfight. Most were unarmed. According to KilledByPolice.net, more than 3,087 have been murdered since 2013. By the time you read this, the number of dead will have climbed higher and higher. But no one can measure the full extent of this dizzying spiral of violence, because no federal-level, comprehensive database on how many Americans are killed by law enforcement exists. FBI Director James Comey told reporters, "It's ridiculous I can't tell you how many people were shot by police in this country, last week, last year, the last decade."

Alongside this theft of life are the smaller thefts of money, time and bodily integrity. Police enact a kind of ghetto tax, which traps the Black poor in a downward spiral. Every time I come home, I see a pair of cops on the corner. And every summer, the NYPD erects surveillance towers in Bedford-Stuyvesant, Brooklyn. And when my neighbors talk, they often tell stories of tickets they got for traffic stops, drinking on the stoop or just riding a bicycle on the sidewalk.

In report after report, we see police departments run like giant vacuum cleaners over poor, Black neighborhoods, sucking money from people who have little to begin with. In 2010, The Village Voice published "The Blue Tapes," showing NYPD cops being told by superiors to "pay the rent" by ticketing and arresting people for minor offenses. A thousand miles away, the US Department of Justice investigated the Ferguson, Missouri, police. It released a report saying that local law enforcement jacked up fines, used excessive force against Black people and essentially ran "debtors' prisons" where people were jailed for not paying tickets. On August 25, 2014, Democracy Now! interviewed a man named George Fields as he waited in line for the funeral of Michael Brown, the Black teenager killed by former Ferguson police officer Darren Wilson. He said, "It's just a little too much when you get pulled over for menial things. You have to go through too much to get out, and you lose your jobs and what not, you know, for a $50 ticket and pull-over."[2]

And then there is the theft of one's body. In city after city, police stop young men of color, frisk them and leave them seething with fear and rage. The cops' handprints stain one's skin. NYPD officers have stopped and frisked 5 million New Yorkers since 2002; most were Black and Latino men. Only now, after pressure, has the practice been relaxed. In Philadelphia, the American Civil Liberties Union (ACLU) published a report showing that since 2011, roughly 200,000 people have been stopped, and nearly 90 percent of the frisks were, again, of young people of color. Imagine living your adolescence in terror of being picked up, hassled, groped and bullied by men who can kill you.

Whether it's on the books or not, cops across the country practice racial profiling and stop-and-frisk. In 2014, NYPD Commissioner William Bratton told CBS, "Every police department in America does it. The challenge is to do it constitutionally within the law ... compassionately; you're dealing with human beings." But the humanity of those being stopped and frisked is already forfeited when they are profiled instantly as a problem. And this is condoned because the police are not creating racism but reflecting it. A larger implicit social consensus rules the city, a dominant narrative that Black and Latino youth, specifically males, are a danger. If not checked, the story goes, they will band together in wolf packs and roam the streets to mug, rape and murder. And often we, people of color, internalize this imagery until a pain shocks us out of our double consciousness and we see the true source of danger.

Months after Bratton's CBS interview, I sat with Chavis and asked about her son. "The school he went to was rough; kids were selling drugs," she said. "The police beat the crap out of this one kid and no one said anything." Her voice seemed to punch the air with anger.

"My son was stopped by cops a lot," Chavis said. "He felt powerless and depressed. I told him it was how he dressed." She looked at me. "I don't believe that today," she said.

Killing the Future

"I believe that children are our future," the girl sang on stage in the Bed-Stuy park, pushing her voice to sound like pop diva Whitney Houston. "Teach them well and let them lead the way." I smiled and covered my mouth as my friend nudged me. When she finished, we applauded. As we left, my friend joked, "Well, do you think children are the future?" I looked at him like he was crazy, as if to say, of course they are. He shrugged. "I never felt like the future," he said.

Decades ago, Martin Luther King Jr. described a girl learning about segregation in his "Letter From Birmingham Jail," seeing, he wrote, "ominous clouds of inferiority beginning to form in her little mental sky." More than 50 years later, I see whiteness like a roving vortex that steals childhood. I see it in the kids on my block, watching police arrest their parents. In New York alone, 120,000 Black men are missing from families; they're locked in jail or they died early. The number goes up to 1.5 million Black men gone nationwide. I see it in how children gather on corners to recreate a family after theirs was ripped apart. I see it in how they taunt each other for being too dark, too nappy or too poor. And I see it in a CBS report about "hood disease," a tacky name for the fact that Black kids in poor areas have post-traumatic stress disorder. They see so many shootings and fights that they are walking in a constant state of despair and rage.

And trauma freezes the soul, which is why as time moves forward, so many Black children fall behind. They are punished more harshly and expelled more quickly. In major cities, only 60 percent of Black males graduate high school. Stranded in the streets, those boys are profiled as older, as a threat, as possibly carrying a weapon. When cops bully them, scare them, fuck with them, it's because our children aren't seen as part of the future. Our children are disposable.

Standing on my stoop and seeing kids play, knowing the history they emerged from and the dangers they face, I wonder how many of them we will lose. And thinking of my hand in that rusted slave shackle many years ago, I wonder about the very first of us chained to this world. How many have we lost? How many of us have been killed by whiteness? How many dead thrown into the sea or buried on plantations, hanged or burned alive, raped or jailed? How many millions upon millions?

Can those lives be redeemed? Here in America? Around us is a nation taught to see us first as semi-animals, now criminals; it's a vision produced from social conflict where the very idea of crime is a political tool the elites use to hammer the poor.

HSBC bankers can launder drug money for Mexican cartels without fear of punishment, while Michael Brown is targeted by Darren Wilson for walking in the street and shot dead. But underneath the conflict view of crime as a political concept, there is still a social-consensus view of crime based on innate human empathy, especially for children. So when Trayvon Martin, Michael Brown or Emmett Till are killed, all young Black men, all innocent, it forces the nation to confront one set of values with another. In that flash of contradiction, everything can be seen.

Into the moment of visibility we march. But when we do, we march into the streets to move the people to confront the state itself. We know from the evidence of our lives and from academic reports like "Testing Theories of American Politics: Elites, Interest Groups, and Average Citizens" by Martin Gilens and Benjamin I. Page[3] that our democracy is controlled by a wealthy elite. Politicians who work for the wealthy need the police to protect them from the people. And so the whole chain of command protects the killer cop. The ruling class give carte blanche to law enforcement, who in turn press down on those most stranded by the neoliberal state, the poor—and more so, the Black poor.

We march against the state, but also, inevitably, into it. Our struggle has been for the recognition of our humanity in a flawed democracy, one split between the universal value of human freedom and white ethnic nationalism. We had to give ourselves to the universal, and that means that Black Lives Matter stands for large-scale transformation. If we win, our victory means an end to the drug war. It means abolishing the police state and ending the very source of crime, which is poverty itself.

But we've only won half-victories, and even those are gutted out. In the midst of protest, the question stands before us: How do we redeem our dead and the dead parts of ourselves? How do we end this centuries-old vortex of whiteness, ripping us apart? The one thing that is knowable is that the end of racism has to free us all or it will free no one.

Gregory

"Tell me how your son died," I asked. It was toward the end of our interview. Chavis and I were in our own bubble in the café, oblivious to everyone else. She took a breath. "He was caught in crossfire on the street," Chavis said. "His friends tried to take him to the hospital, but police pulled them over and ordered them to put him down on the ground." She took a moment and looked away. "They never called an ambulance. He bled to death a block away from the hospital."

My own heart hurt. Imagining this young man, whom this strong woman gave birth to, dying in a puddle of his own blood as cops stood and ignored his pain. I wanted to meet her son and laugh with him, get to know him. You can feel the imprint of people you never met in the way others talk about them, the way family caresses their memory like a pearl. Hearing Chavis remember her son, I could tell he was a good kid, deeply loved.

"What do you miss about your son?" I asked. She half-smiled. "His laughter and how protective he was over his sisters." She rocked back and forth for a second. "You know, the night he was killed, when I was asleep, I tried to get up but felt a weight on my chest. I think it was my son telling me what was happening to him, you know, that he couldn't get up.

"Some families never recover. I know mothers on drugs. Fathers who are alcoholics," she said. "A child's death creates a division in the family. Some just want to let it go. They're hurt, depressed. Others want to fight until they get justice. My youngest didn't take it very well."

"How so?" I put down my pen.

"She would sit up," Chavis said, "and look out the window, waiting for him to come home."

2.

Ring of Snitches: How Detroit Police Slapped False Murder Convictions on Young Black Men[1]

Aaron Miguel Cantú

It was the middle of July in 1994, outside an old strip club on Detroit's West Side, when Lonnie Bell admitted to his friend Christopher Brooks that he had killed somebody.

The two young men, both drug dealers, had been friends for a year. Less than a week earlier, while Brooks was selling crack outside of a laundromat on the East Side, he'd happened to see Bell leaving a home where police later discovered the body of Willa B. Bias, shot to death. Brooks casually mentioned what he'd seen as the two of them relaxed in the strip club. According to Brooks, Bell was mum at first but then invited Brooks to blow lines of cocaine in his Ford Bronco. Inside the car, Bell confessed to the murder.

He said he killed Bias, possibly for the $70,000 in drug money her foster son kept hidden in the basement. He also told Brooks that if he ever told anyone what he'd seen, he'd lay Brooks' corpse next to the woman's. Brooks was so shaken—Bell had a reputation as a cold, careful killer—that he soon decamped for Monroe, Michigan, fearing Bell would kill him if he stayed in Detroit. Brooks says he never told anybody what he saw until 2013, the year he was contacted by an independent investigator reassessing the murder case. Brooks says he is coming forward now because he believes the wrong man is in prison for Bias' death.

Today, Lonnie Bell is dead, a casualty of Detroit's gang warfare. The man imprisoned for Bias' murder is Lacino Hamilton, her foster son, who grew up in her home and was 19 years old when she was killed. Hamilton, now 40, has always maintained his innocence and says he loved his foster mother—whom he simply refers to as "Mom." Without a retrial, the earliest he can expect to be let out of prison is 2046, when he will be 71.

Hamilton's murder conviction hinged on two pieces of evidence: a coerced statement and testimony from a jailhouse informant claiming that Hamilton confessed to the murder while awaiting trial in his jail cell. But according to affidavits, courthouse transcripts, letters and internal memos obtained by Truthout, the informant—who is long deceased—may have received incentives from Detroit police to falsely testify against a number of individuals. These documents also suggest that the informant was part of a ring of jailhouse informants—or "snitches"—that allegedly received lenient sentences as well as food, drugs, sex and special privileges from detectives in the Detroit Police Department's homicide division in return for making statements against dozens of prisoners eventually convicted of murder.

Jailhouse Informants "Lie Primarily in Exchange for Lenience"

A 2005 report published by the Northwestern University School of Law[2] traced the first documented use of "snitch testimony" in the United States to 1819, when the state of Vermont convicted Jesse Boorn for murder based on testimony from his cellmate. The cellmate told a judge that Boorn confessed to the crime inside their jail cell while awaiting his trial. In exchange for testifying, the cellmate was freed after Boorn's trial, and Boorn was sentenced to the gallows.

This basic reward system underpinning jailhouse informant testimony persists into the present day. It's not difficult to imagine why a prisoner-informant would lie about overhearing a confession when it means real material benefits.

"Informants lie primarily in exchange for lenience for their own crimes, although sometimes they lie for money," according to a report from Golden Gate University Law Review.[3] While informants are motivated to falsify testimony for material reward, prosecutors are often motivated to make those informants sound believable to a judge. Testimony from a single jailhouse informant is enough to convict a person for a charge as serious as murder, according to Valerie Newman, assistant defender in Michigan's State Appellate Defender Office.

"You can be convicted on any credible evidence ruled as admissible," she told Truthout. "If a judge rules it's admissible and a jury believes it, you can be convicted. People find it hard to believe people can be sent to prison for the rest of their lives based on this kind of testimony."

They can also be killed. The Northwestern report found that snitch testimony was paramount in 45.9 percent of 111 death row exonerations since the late 1970s, making it the leading cause of wrongful convictions in US capital cases. As DNA detection became more sophisticated in the late 1990s, waves of prisoners were exonerated, and some states began examining their use of jailhouse informants. The Innocence Project, a group that investigates innocence claims in decades-old cases, claims that in 15 percent of all wrongful conviction cases overturned by DNA testing, statements from people with incentives to testify were critical evidence used to convict a person.[4]

These revelations have moved some states to examine the use of jailhouse informant testimony. In a broad review of all state defendants wrongfully convicted of capital murder, the Illinois Commission on Capital Punishment found that prosecution often "relied unduly on the uncorroborated testimony of a witness with something to gain," including "in-custody informants,"[5] and passed a law preventing death sentences if a conviction was based on the "uncorroborated testimony of an accomplice or a jail-house snitch." Similarly,

California reopened 225 cases in 1989 after an informant blew the lid off the way Los Angeles prosecutors fed prewritten testimonies to informants, and the state later adopted a law requiring that informant testimony be held to higher proof standards.[6]

Whistleblower in the Homicide Division

While these higher standards can sometimes backfire in states like California,[7] in other states like Michigan, where there are no regulations for using informant testimony beyond prosecutors knowing and admitting to it, there has never been a serious investigation into the systematic use of jailhouse informants by police and prosecutors. Claudia Whitman, director of the National Death Row Assistance Network (NDRAN), believes some cases would be overturned following a serious re-examination.

"In the two cases [from Detroit] I have worked on in depth, jailhouse informants were major players in the state obtaining convictions," she told Truthout, acknowledging that while using informant testimony is not illegal, it is known to be highly inaccurate.

On at least one occasion, the veneer of secrecy over the Detroit Police Department's homicide division was punctured, giving a fleeting glimpse of systemic corruption. In 1997, Detroit native Dwight Carl Love was freed from a Michigan prison after 15 years.[8] He was exonerated not by DNA tests but through the efforts of a tenacious defense attorney named Sarah Hunter and a whistleblower inside Detroit's homicide unit. Based on a tip from the whistleblower, Hunter forced Detroit police to turn over evidence they'd hidden from trial that supported Love's innocence. He was exonerated—as other men would be in later years[9]—because of the police department's failure to present exculpatory evidence to the court.

According to an affidavit from Hunter, the whistleblower, who allegedly committed suicide less than a year after meeting the attorney,[10] told Hunter that police routinely hid exculpatory evidence from prosecutors and judges. In the years after Hunter obtained the Love evidence, she claimed to Claudia Whitman that Detroit police intimidated her by beating prisoners if they spoke to her. Neither she nor the police responded to Truthout's request for comment.

Snitches on the Ninth Floor

Besides the attorney and the whistleblower, evidence of systemic corruption within Detroit's homicide unit in the mid-1990s comes from some of the alleged informants themselves. Their claims involve dozens of cases of men who are still in prisons across Michigan.

Before Jonathan Hewitt was sentenced to four years in prison in 1994, he says he spent months in a cell on the ninth floor of the Detroit Police Department waiting for his trial. While he was there, he claims, homicide detectives offered him and at least six other prisoners food and drink, conjugal visits, time to watch television, and, most importantly, the promise of lenient sentences if they testified against other prisoners also being held in the jail cells on the ninth floor. Hewitt says police told informants that a deal for their reduced sentences would be hatched after the suspect's trial, so that they would not have to acknowledge it in court, which could have swayed jurors away from a conviction.

"The Detectives would provide me with the necessary information, but just they wanted me to try and convince a couple prisoners to tell me about their cases—murder [cases] only," Hewitt wrote in an affidavit in 2011. In a phone interview with Truthout, he said detectives supplied him and other informants with prewritten statements to memorize before the preliminary hearings of the accused men. In those statements, informants would say that the accused person confessed to their crime in a way that "filled in" the details detectives were missing to connect the suspect to their crime. Often, Hewitt said, informants had familial or fraternal connections to the men they snitched on, indicating they were all scooped up from the same underclass milieu.

It's hard to gauge how many cases from that time relied on informant testimony, and how critically. Hewitt estimated that between just two informants he personally knew, upward of 30 men were convicted of murder in the mid-1990s. By another account, from Detroit Police Sgt. Dale Collins in the homicide division, a single informant helped police with at least 20 cases before July 1994.

In 2013, a defense attorney looking into a prisoner's innocence claim hired a private attorney to interview another admitted snitch in 1994, Edward Allen. Allen told the investigator that police witnesses on the ninth floor of the Detroit Police Department were allowed visitors who brought food and drugs from outside, and claimed he even had sex with one of the homicide detectives. He also revealed in a letter to a federal circuit judge that he spent two years imprisoned on the ninth floor and hoped to extract a favorable plea deal for helping police with five different cases.

Allen estimated in another letter to Larry Smith, a man convicted largely because of Allen's testimony, that over 100 people convicted of murder were "set up" by Detroit police based on false informant testimony. He also admitted to falsifying his testimony against Smith, who is still incarcerated. Allen, who is currently incarcerated, was released from prison in 2008 but sentenced to three years in 2012 after violating his probation.

The Memo

Eventually, some of the defense attorneys for men incriminated by snitches approached the Wayne County Prosecutor's Office with concerns about certain informants. In February 1995, the deputy chief assistant prosecutor for Wayne County, Robert Agacinski, wrote to his supervisor expressing concern over the department's use of informants. He noted that two detectives in the homicide department, Dale Collins and Bill Rice, had approached prosecutors to ask that they reduce a sentence for two informants, a request the district attorney turned down.

If an investigation had found that police were promising informants lenient sentences—which is outside of their authority—or working with prosecutors to fabricate informants' testimony, it could have resulted in evidentiary hearings, jump-starting the process of overturning convictions. But Agacinski, who headed the Michigan Attorney Grievance Commission for 14 years,[11] says nothing was ever done to address the concerns he outlined.

"I was low-middle-ranking management. I wasn't part of top level," he told Truthout. "Nobody ever told me anything else and I have no idea if [the memo] was acted upon."

One informant Agacinski mentioned by name in the memo was Lacino Hamilton's snitch, Olivera Rico Cowen, a man living with AIDS. In July 1994, three weeks before Hamilton was arrested for his foster mother's murder, Cowen was granted a radically reduced sentence for cooperating with homicide detectives. Instead of serving five to 15 years in prison, he would only have to do a year—as long as he continued to cooperate with homicide investigators.

But Cowen didn't live that long. He spent the last months of his life on the ninth floor of the police department, loyally trying to coerce a confession out of Hamilton.

"Reading and Rebelling"

Lacino Hamilton rejects the legitimacy of the entire carceral system and says his resistance to the system's dictates has likely made his life harder in his current prison, the already-violent Kinross Correctional Facility. Over the last 19 years, Hamilton has bounced from prison to prison before finally ending up at Kinross, near the Canadian border.

"I don't know how to reconcile or accept this. I just don't know how, so I don't try," he told Truthout, adding that he spent much of his time "reading and rebelling."

Even after nearly two decades of imprisonment, Hamilton rages against prisons, police and a whole social order founded on oppression.

"How some of us live is not a mistake; neither is it the product of a broken system," he wrote in an essay from prison. "We live like that because it is profitable to a lot of people and businesses: pawn shops, payday loan services, slum lords, creditors, social services, and others who traffic in misery."[12]

These days, Hamilton has reason to feel optimistic. After writing to thousands of journalists, lawyers and colleges to plead his case, he finally got in touch with Claudia Whitman from NDRAN, who supplied this reporter with most of the documents behind this story. Whitman also made contact with Christopher Brooks, the prisoner who says he knows who really killed Hamilton's foster mother. With Whitman's help, Hamilton was able to convince an up-and-coming attorney, Marty Chartier, to work to overturn his conviction pro bono. Chartier says her firm vetted the case before taking it on.

"If we think someone is wrongfully convicted, we really put the resources of the firm behind the client," she told Truthout. "If we're going to take on this case for free, it means we really believe in it."

Hamilton was imprisoned with a man named Darnell Thompson, who claims he was threatened by police into pinning the crime on Hamilton. In an affidavit reviewed by Truthout, Thompson said that homicide detectives and prisoner Olivera Rico Cowen conspired to pressure him into testifying against Hamilton. Thompson, who was 18 at the time, says he was coerced into signing a statement against Hamilton, but he later refused to testify against Hamilton in court. Still, Thompson's statement, along with Cowen's testimony and testimony about Hamilton's character by a neighbor, were enough for a jury to convict. Hamilton was sentenced to 50 to 80 years in prison, as well as two years for a felony firearm charge.

Chartier says Cowen's testimony was a critical reason for the conviction, even though he was also instrumental in six other murder convictions, according to court documents.

Patterns and Practices

Documents pertinent to Hamilton's case also suggest there may be many more prisoners in Michigan convicted because of the Detroit Police Department's jailhouse informants. They include Larry Smith, the man to whom informant Edward Allen admitted falsifying testimony in a 2002 letter.

Like Hamilton, Smith wrote to lawyers and journalists for years before somebody responded. When he was 18, he claims, he was detained for murder without an attorney, which he says allowed police to fabricate a statement by him. Allen later corroborated that fabricated statement at Smith's trial. Smith's current attorney, Mary Owens, says they are wading through the appeals process now.

"In many cases, even if all the witnesses have recanted, or if a person claims innocence, it's still difficult to [overturn a conviction]," she told Truthout. "The courts are more concerned with whether the trial has been procedurally proper."

But in recent years, as challenges to the police as an institution have risen in US media and on the streets, the Department of Justice (DOJ) has more publicly scrutinized police across the country, most memorably in Ferguson.[13] Ron Scott, director of the Detroit Coalition Against Police Brutality, is hopeful that the old snitch cases in Detroit could be reviewed by the DOJ, given its recent investigations.

"If we could find those patterns and practices, [the DOJ] would be willing to use it as a template for looking at the department and the way it infuses this behavior," he said, adding that he and a federal monitor had met with prisoners from Detroit with "questionable convictions."

Yet even if federal investigators do get involved, legal sources tell Truthout any lawsuit that follows would likely only affect future policies and practices, not grant relief for currently incarcerated people alleging past harm.

Backdrop of Corruption

Federal intervention in Detroit police affairs would not be new; in fact, the police there have been under a federal "consent decree," which is the DOJ's official method of addressing civil rights abuses by law enforcement. Police under a consent decree are audited every quarter by a court-appointed monitor to assess their progress on reforms. Detroit's decree was put into effect after the Detroit Free Press exposed that Detroit had the highest number of fatal shootings by police in the United States.[14]

Despite the pretense of oversight, in 2008 the FBI uncovered a romantic affair between the federal monitor and the city's now-imprisoned mayor, Kwame Kilpatrick. The monitor and her team were replaced in 2009 by the current monitor, Robert Warshaw. The city will exit the decree in 2016.

In addition to the affair scandal, evidence of corruption in the homicide department emerged in 2008. An audit by Michigan State Police into the Detroit department's crime lab revealed that police made assumptions about "the entirety of all items [in a case] based on the analysis of only a few," likely resulting in erroneous convictions.[15] The lab's closure led to yet another scandal three years later: The Detroit Free Press discovered that the lab, and all the evidence in it, including sealed evidence bags, ballistic tests and investigative reports, had simply been abandoned and left open to anybody who wanted to go inside. Evidence touching hundreds of cases was allowed to degrade.[16]

Neglect

Lacino Hamilton was part of a generation that grew up in the so-called crack era, and before going to prison he sold drugs in order to build a life for himself in a dying city. As in Congress and in major cities across the country, Detroit's answer to the social fallout of drugs and poverty was more aggressive policing and sentencing. It fell to homicide detectives during the lockup craze of the mid-1990s to funnel Black youth from the streets into the prison system.

Around the time when the snitch ring on the ninth floor was busiest, Detroit police were casting a wide net over entire neighborhoods that bore the worst effects of divestment and disrepair. This is, in fact, how Hamilton describes his arrest: He wasn't singled out after his foster mother's murder but happened to be picked up alongside many other young Black men after she was killed. He was originally questioned in an unrelated case before detectives allegedly pinned the murder on him, when they couldn't pin it on another suspect.

Hamilton says the reason his original defense attorney did not challenge the prosecutor's use of an informant corresponds to some of the reasons Black communities around the nation still suffer at the hands of the state: neglect and an assumption of disposability.

"By now, the demonstrative wasting away of Black life in urban areas, such as Detroit, has become an historical and social fact, called neglect," he wrote in an email to Truthout. "I mean what else can it be? Society places little to no value on Black lives. And what people don't value, they don't bother with ... I'm in prison because no one wondered, cared, or took the time to ask how a handful of serial offenders [snitches] could show up in court again and again to have received unsolicited confessions—neglect."

3.

Amid Shootings, Chicago Police Department Upholds Culture of Impunity[1]

Sarah Macaraeg and Alison Flowers

On a clear, warm April day in 2013, a 35-year-old father of two, Ortiz Glaze, was manning a grill in his South Chicago neighborhood. He was cooking seafood, chicken and potatoes for scores of guests, including kids, in a parking lot. The barbecue, which stretched from day to night, was to commemorate his friend who had recently died from a shooting.

A group of Chicago Police Department (CPD) officers pulled up to the party, some wearing plain clothes and driving unmarked cars.

What happened next is where the stories differ. Police officers say Glaze was holding a cup that appeared to contain alcohol, ignoring orders, and gesturing to his waistband, where Officer Louis Garcia and his partner, Officer Jeffrey Jones, say they believed he stowed a gun.

The other version is one corroborated by witnesses—that Jones fired into the crowd upon approach, causing everyone, including Glaze, to run away.

From there, the following facts are not in dispute: Glaze, who had no criminal record, was unarmed. No gun was recovered. And while he was running away with his back to police, Jones and Garcia fired multiple shots at him, hitting him twice.

Glaze lived to tell his story.

"I laid there scared," Glaze said of the moment when the bullets hit him. "Then he stood over me with his gun. I didn't know if he was going to shoot at me again."

When Glaze fell to the ground, his left arm and thigh wounded, Garcia handcuffed his right hand to his belt loop, arrested him and sent him to the hospital for treatment.

"My arm was a jangle," Glaze said, pointing to the scar on his arm and the surgical plate beneath his flesh.

The officers fingerprinted Glaze, handcuffed his good hand to his hospital bed and used patient restraints to tie his foot to the bed rail. They interrogated him.

After the shooting, a felony review unit at the Cook County State's Attorney's Office did not charge Glaze. The officers instead pursued charges of lesser misdemeanor offenses, including aggravated assault and resisting and obstructing police.

At Glaze's bench trial almost a year later, it was the word of five police officers against Glaze. The judge quickly acquitted him of the charges.

"The judge saw right through them," Glaze said. "It lets you know that they was lying."

Glaze filed a lawsuit in April 2014 suing the City of Chicago, the Chicago Police Department and a slew of named officers, including Jones and Garcia. The lawsuit claims police planted a silver cell phone on Glaze—what police say resembled a gun as he was running—to justify their shooting. The device did not show up during an initial inventory report of Glaze's belongings, according to the lawsuit. The CPD did not respond to Truthout's requests for comment on behalf of the department and named officers in this story.

Today Glaze, who is unemployed, keeps to himself and doesn't go out much.

"I'm not the person like I was," he said. "I'm just not really coming back around. Only time I can kick it is when I'm out of town. When I'm in Chicago, I can't be myself."

"Quasi-Military Organizations"

Glaze was one of 43 people shot by Chicago police in 2013. Thirteen of those were killed, according to Chicago's Independent Police Review Authority (IPRA), the agency that reviews officer-involved shootings. IPRA did not respond to Truthout's requests for comment.

"Police departments are quasi-military organizations," said Art Lurigio, a criminologist and clinical psychologist who teaches at Loyola University. "The police are authorized to use force in ways that no other citizen is authorized to act."

The officer who shot at Glaze multiple times—Louis Garcia—has shot before. A May 2006 news release from the CPD shows that Garcia and his former partner, Martin Teresi, shot an armed offender in 2005. The CPD awarded the pair the Superintendent's Award of Valor for the shooting.

"Police are rewarded for exercising force and sometimes engaging in violent behaviors, including shooting at the suspects, including shooting dead the suspects, including tasing the suspects," Lurigio said. "They are not credited for performance that's passive."

According to a new report by the Chicago organization We Charge Genocide,[2] presented to the United Nations Committee Against Torture in November 2014 (see Chapter 11), more than 75 percent of those shot by Chicago police from 2009 to 2013 were Black. African-Americans are 10 times more likely to be shot by police than white people, IPRA data show.

A two-month investigation by Truthout delved into police shootings and misconduct complaints in Chicago, uncovering several key facts that raise questions about deadly force and police impunity.[3]

The investigation matched data on officers who had a high volume of historic misconduct complaints with police unit designations and current City of Chicago employee and budgetary public data. Alongside researching public documents, such as legal complaints and police news releases, the investigation was able to track the position of alleged repeat abusers still on the force and study the city's investment in their conduct by way of salary, overtime pay and settlements.

To identify police shooters in controversial cases, Truthout cross-referenced media accounts naming victims with corresponding civil suits naming officers, screening hundreds of documents.

Reporters also interviewed victims of police brutality, criminologists, lawyers and a retired police officer, in addition to Jamie Kalven of the Invisible Institute, a Chicago-based journalistic production company that led the seven-year battle to make misconduct complaint data public.

Two Freedom of Information Act (FOIA) requests submitted to the CPD for Tactical Response Reports[4]—the primary source documents created by the CPD in any incident where an officer discharges a firearm—were rejected, even when the second request was narrowed to cover just six specific officers and three specific dates and locations.

The investigation found that at least 21 CPD officers are currently serving on the force, some with honors, after shooting citizens under highly questionable circumstances, resulting in at least $30.2 million in taxpayer-funded City of Chicago settlements thus far.

Six officers who have shot and killed civilians also have a large volume of unpenalized complaints of misconduct.

At least 500 CPD officers with more than 10 misconduct complaints over a five-year period (2001–2006) are still serving on the force. Their combined salary is $42.5 million dollars.

Four lieutenants, the director and an organizer of the Chicago Alternative Policing Strategy (CAPS), 55 detectives, a field training officer, and 69 sergeants are among the 500 CPD officers with more than 10 misconduct complaints over the five-year period.

Police officer Raymond Piwnicki, now a detective, had the highest number of complaints in the five-year period, with 55 misconduct complaints and zero penalties. Piwnicki was awarded the Superintendent's Award of Valor in 2013—for a shooting as a result of which he is now a defendant in a civil suit that cites his "deliberate indifference" to a fellow officer's deadly force.

More than 60 of the 662 police officers with at least 10 misconduct complaints hailed from the Special Operations Section, which was responsible for 1,311 complaints in these five years of data alone. An elite citywide unit tasked with drug and gang investigations, Special

Operations was disbanded in 2007 amid multiple corruption scandals, which not only resulted in criminal charges of armed robbery, aggravated kidnapping and home invasion being brought against seven of its former members—two are now in jail—but also yielded a guilty plea in a murder for hire scheme. It was replaced by the Mobile Strike Force one year later, in the same unit headquarters, with the same orders and many of the same officers. Mobile Strike Force was itself disbanded in 2011, but Mayor Rahm Emanuel reactivated it in 2013 with orders to "smother outbreaks of violence," according to the Chicago Sun-Times.

From 2002 to 2008, out of 90 excessive force complaints specifically denoting improper "weapon, use/display of," all but eight were dismissed, with only five noting the violation. During this time period, a paralyzed man, Cornelius Ware, was shot and killed by Officer Anthony Blake, whose record noted a weapon complaint as "unfounded." The City of Chicago later awarded Ware's family a settlement of $5.25 million.

During the 2001 to 2006 span, more than three dozen police officers had 29 or more misconduct complaints on their records, more than double the number of complaints accumulated by indicted Chicago police commander Glenn Evans during the same period.

"Full-Time Gangsters"

Martin Teresi, former partner of Louis Garcia, who shot Ortiz Glaze, accumulated 35 misconduct complaints in the five years prior to his and Garcia's 2006 award. Those complaints resulted in zero penalties.

"The data we have would suggest conditions of virtual impunity for abusive officers," said writer and human rights activist Jamie Kalven of the Invisible Institute. "That means full-time gangsters. That means utterly cruel individuals who get off on humiliating African-Americans or women. A small amount on the force, but a huge impact."

Among the complaints against Teresi are two different excessive force complaints involving the teen children of Black officers, one of whom suffered a fractured nose and two broken ribs, according to the complaint, which was settled out of court.

Since the 2001–2006 time period, Teresi has been named in another excessive force complaint involving minors, and in the settlement of Mario Navia Jr., whose complaint describes being pulled over without reason and then quickly arrested, pepper-sprayed and beaten by six officers who used a nightstick that left a gash in his head requiring multiple staples.

That case was settled in 2013. In 2014, Teresi received the Superintendent's Award of Valor from the Chicago Police Department, for another incident involving the discharge of his weapon, according to the department's news release.

Garcia's record from 2001 to 2006 did not exceed 10 complaints, the baseline for inclusion in the repeat-misconduct-complaint list. Yet civil suits against Garcia—there are three in progress, including that of Glaze—mark a consistent history of extreme excessive force prior to Glaze's shooting.

In 2005, Ronald Johnson, from Chicago's South Side, brought a lawsuit against Garcia, seven other officers and the City of Chicago, alleging excessive force, false arrest, unreasonable search and seizure, malicious prosecution and hate crime.

Garcia is described as solely responsible for the hate crime of "placing Johnson in a choke-hold which cut off his breathing. The officer repeatedly called Mr. Johnson a n-gger" and "threatened to kill Mr. Johnson," according to the lawsuit.

Johnson's case settled for $99,000.

Five years later, a charge of excessive force was again filed against Garcia. The lawsuit, made by disabled 52-year-old Ruben Sanchez, describes Garcia as emerging from an unmarked police car, gun drawn, in front of Sanchez's home. Ordered to lie on his stomach, Sanchez explained he could not comply given a recent surgery. "Garcia punched Sanchez in the mouth," the civil suit alleges, further elaborating, "When Sanchez, now bloodied, insisted he could not lie on his stomach, Garcia again punched Sanchez in the mouth and forcibly threw Sanchez to the ground."

Three years after the Sanchez incident, Garcia and Jeffrey Jones shot at Ortiz Glaze.

"A Biopsy of the City's Accountability System"

In 2014, a watershed moment in police accountability occurred, opening a small window that has shed light on CPD patterns and practices.

In March, an Illinois appeals court ruled in Kalven v. Chicago that documents bearing on allegations of police misconduct are public information. In July, the City of Chicago released sets of documents long sought by lawyers and journalists.

The sunshine is thanks in large part to Jamie Kalven, who had previously become entangled, and later intervened, in a federal lawsuit where the police records were at issue.

"The dramatic portraits that emerge are of individual officers, but it's also a biopsy of the city's accountability system," Kalven said of the now-public police data. "There are patterns that jump out to you."

Out of the approximately 12,000 officers on the Chicago force between 2001 and 2006, most officers saw between zero and two misconduct complaints, Kalven said. Another set of officers had between two and 10 complaints.

But where the data points indicate a troubling pattern is the 662 officers who individually account for 10 misconduct complaints or more—what Kalven calls the "repeater list."[5]

Shootings

The CPD's track record of rarely delivering meaningful penalties for misconduct signals a culture in which incidents of fatal force are nearly always deemed justifiable.

There is one notable exception: the case of Officer Dante Servin, who in 2015 stood trial for shooting Rekia Boyd in the back of the head while off duty in 2012, killing her. On April 20, 2015, Servin was acquitted of charges of involuntary manslaughter, reckless discharge of a firearm and reckless conduct, though many activists and legal experts—perhaps even the judge in his case—believe he should have been charged with murder.[6] Nevertheless, Servin was the first CPD officer in 15 years to stand criminal trial.

As for the many remaining officers who have likewise shot civilians—shootings deemed justified under highly questionable circumstances—it is nearly impossible to track the consequences of such impunity.

City agencies have blocked efforts to monitor the frequency of officer-involved shootings. In 2014 John Conroy, director of investigations at the DePaul Legal Clinic (and the journalist who helped expose the decades-long CPD torture ring that operated under former Cmdr. Jon Burge), submitted several public-information requests seeking records related to the frequency of police shootings. The Office of the Mayor, the Chicago Police Board and IPRA all responded that no such records existed, while the Chicago Police Department turned over a cursory two-page document that illuminated little or nothing.

Kalven's "biopsy" of city data—compiled after a long fight for information by civil rights lawyers—confirms that the city does not track shootings, perform pattern analyses of shootings, or examine officers and units with high numbers of misconduct complaints in a short period of time.

Officer Gildardo Sierra

In 2011, CPD Superintendent Garry McCarthy, speaking with the Chicago Tribune, confirmed the department did not maintain any internal system to track officers involved in multiple shootings. In a span of six months that same year, Officer Gildardo Sierra shot three people—two of them fatally.

Flint Farmer was the last of those shot by Sierra, who had been called on a domestic disturbance to Farmer's Englewood location. When Sierra and his partner arrived, Farmer took off running. At the next block, Sierra, who later claimed he "feared for his life," began shooting at Farmer, who was unarmed. Discharging his weapon a total of 16 times, Sierra hit Farmer with seven of his bullets. It was the final three shots that killed Farmer, according to the Cook County medical examiner.

A patrol car video shows Sierra walking in a semicircle around Farmer, who is lying face down on the ground, wounded, before firing three shots into his back, killing him. The shots are illuminated in the video by muzzle flashes indicative of close range.[7]

Farmer's family settled their civil suit for $4.1 million.

Yet Cook County State's Attorney Anita Alvarez ruled the shooting justified. After a two-year investigation, county prosecutors concluded that evidence supported Sierra's claim that he had acted in self-defense—after mistaking Farmer's cellphone for a weapon.

"Not every mistake demands the action of the criminal justice system, even when the results are tragic," Alvarez wrote in a letter to McCarthy.

Stripped of police powers, Sierra was transferred to the city's 311 call center.

Near the beginning of his career on the force, Sierra had been awarded the Distinguished Service Award by the Fraternal Order of Police. At the City Council Finance Committee meeting in which the settlement was approved, Leslie Darling, an attorney for the City of Chicago, told council members Farmer's shooting was in fact the eighth in which Sierra was involved.

City data lists Sierra as a police officer with a salary of $78,012.

Still on the Force

Truthout's investigation identified a number of additional officers who have pulled the trigger in instances of highly controversial civilian deaths.[8] Including officers already mentioned herein, the investigation revealed that, among officers currently serving on the force, at least five have shot and killed civilians from behind, and each has a record of more than 10 misconduct complaints in five years.

Among this group is Officer John Fitzgerald, who shot Aaron Harrison, a black 18-year-old, in 2007, after garnering 25 misconduct complaints between 2001 and 2006. A member of Special Operations, Fitzgerald was awarded the Superintendent's Award of Valor in 2010, according to a CPD news release, for the incident. The shooting was ruled justified by IPRA, largely based on two pieces of evidence: Fitzgerald's assertion that Harrison was attempting to shoot him while running away, and a gun recovered on the scene. Multiple witnesses asserted Harrison was unarmed. In 2013, Harrison's family's civil suit settled for $8.5 million.

Six officers with a record of more than 10 complaints in five years are named in lawsuits for their involvement in shootings, among them Raymond Piwnicki, as well as Officer Chris Hackett, who according to witnesses ran over 23-year-old Jamaal Moore.

Moore, unarmed and attempting to flee from the officer and his partner after a car chase in Englewood that ended in a crash, was then shot by Hackett's partner Ruth Castelli two times at close range, once in the back. IPRA exonerated the officers despite both a patrol car dashcam video and a gas station surveillance video that contradict their account, according to a memorandum opinion and order by the judge in the subsequent civil suit, which settled for $1.25 million. From 2001 to 2006, Hackett garnered 15 misconduct complaints and zero penalties.

Fourteen officers without a record of more than 10 misconduct complaints also fatally shot civilians between 2001 and 2006, including Castelli and Phyllis Clinkscales, who shot unarmed 17-year-old Robert Washington at such close range that residue and the muzzle imprint of her weapon were left on his skin.

The CPD found the shooting justified within hours and later ignored IPRA's recommendation that Clinkscales be fired. In-depth Chicago Tribune reporting in 2007 revealed many other salient facts surrounding the shooting. Yet city data lists Clinkscales as a police officer, with a salary of $83,706 and 2013 overtime earnings of $38,996.

Collis Underwood, whom the City Council granted an honorific resolution this April for intervening in a potentially deadly domestic disturbance, fatally shot 23-year-old Xavier Ferguson twice in the chest following a traffic stop in 2010. Underwood, on patrol in the Mobile Strike Force at the time of the shooting, asserted Ferguson "lunged" for his weapon. Ferguson's family, who did not believe the young father of two would attempt to disarm an officer, filed a wrongful death suit. The jury ruled in Underwood's favor. Another civil suit against him, with a charge of excessive force, is currently underway. According to the lawsuit, Underwood and his partner extensively beat Dennis Dixon, resulting in a "fractured hand that required surgery, a blunt head injury and multiple bruises/contusions."

"We're Not Dirty Harry"

Outside of Chicago, Richard Greenleaf, a retired Albuquerque police sergeant, teaches criminology at Elmhurst College. He is an expert in police psychology.

Citing the split-second, life-or-death dynamic police operate in, Greenleaf empathizes with police officers who have pulled the trigger. He is one of them.

In 1981, Greenleaf shot and killed an armed robber who was out on bond for an alleged stabbing. The guy turned his gun on him; Greenleaf responded by firing three rounds, hitting him twice—once in the chest, and once in the lower groin.

After the incident, he got three days off with pay and had to visit the police counselor. Later, when psychological services had an opening, he became that counselor. Greenleaf holds a graduate degree in counseling and a doctorate in sociology.

Police, whom Greenleaf described as being on high alert and in a constant mindset of danger, talk about "good shootings" and "bad shootings" in such simple terms internally. A "good shooting" is when someone's life was at risk, and a "bad shooting" is what the controversial Ferguson, Missouri, killing of unarmed teenager Michael Brown looks to be, Greenleaf explained.

Greenleaf witnessed abusive force during his seven years as an officer in Albuquerque.

"There are departments that have histories of not just having bad apples, but a batch of rotten apples," Greenleaf said. "But the number of shootings alone does not necessarily mean that the department is corrupt or has bad officers."

Today, Greenleaf says he steers his students, some of them police officers themselves, away from caricatures of law enforcement like Dirty Harry, John Wayne or even Superman.

But when he speaks of taking a human life, his voice lowers and softens.

"I wish it never happened," Greenleaf said. "I wish he had lived. But I was in fear of my life."

However, the aftermath of police shootings in Chicago, Truthout found, contradicts this good shooting/bad shooting dichotomy, with the grisly details behind "good shootings" emerging through video footage, media accounts and civil lawsuits where victims and their families have garnered large settlements. Some of these shootings have not only been "justified" by the CPD, IPRA and former Cook County State's Attorney Anita Alvarez but also rewarded. What remains unknown is the process by which they are judged internally and the systemic underpinnings behind how they come to be praised.

At the same time, no government agency consistently tracks "good shootings" and "bad shootings" among the estimated 1,000 police shootings across the country annually.[9] One of the only attempts includes self-reporting from a fraction of the nation's law enforcement agencies to the FBI's data on "justifiable homicides." A journalist and publisher launched another attempt in 2012, the crowdsourcing project Fatal Encounters. The project seeks to create an impartial, comprehensive and searchable national database of people killed during interactions with law enforcement.[10]

"For Their Reputation"

Chicago's Independent Police Review Authority has conducted 272 investigations of officer-involved shootings over the last five years. Officers are rarely disciplined. In 22 instances, more than one person was shot.

Still, many incidents of police misconduct never make it to IPRA's books because the alleged victims do not complain, leaving only anecdotal evidence recounted to those who will listen. Truthout sought police records to confirm the following accounts—just a few of the many incidents that take place on a daily basis in the city—but the CPD did not respond fully or promptly to these Freedom of Information Act requests.

A 53-year-old South Sider, Percy McGill, has been in and out of prison on drug charges. He claims to be physically handled by police every day.

"They throw you against the car and search you with no reason," McGill said. "I mean, you don't have to be doing anything. You can be just walking down the street, going to the store. If they see you, they're going to stop you and search you."

Andre Wilson, a 51-year-old West Sider, is also no stranger to the criminal justice system, a fact that he believes has caused police to discriminate against him even when he is clean on the streets.

"I've been strip-searched in the middle of the street," Wilson said. "I think that's really degrading."

On one occasion, he flicked a bag of heroin when he saw police coming after him. The bag was never found, "so they found something for me," Wilson said.

Cory Lyles, a 43-year-old father of two from the West Side, does not have a criminal history like McGill or Wilson, but found himself handcuffed to a wall at a police station for hours after being mistaken for someone else.

Once released, Lyles returned to his car to find it doused in Hennessey, he claims. He tried to tell his story to a "white-shirt" back at the station, but never put in a complaint because he felt intimidated by the officers.

Stanley Davis, 45, a West Sider who had only been home from prison for 40 days when he spoke to Truthout in early October, has spent more time incarcerated than free, with seven incarcerations totaling 26 years. He admits he has hustled, but asserts innocence in three of the crimes for which he was imprisoned.

Davis experienced police violence around the 2012 incident that led to his most recent incarceration, he says. After he was stopped and forced to the ground by two officers, a third officer jumped out of his car and came down on his back with his knee, according to Davis.

"It felt like he pushed my back into the earth," Davis said. "I felt that pain for some time, but wasn't nothing broke."

Whether citizens are actually guilty of the perceived offense that leads to apprehension is not what shakes their sense of justice, according to Art Lurigio, criminologist and clinical psychologist at Loyola University.

"More important to citizens than the actual outcome is how they were treated," Lurigio said. "This ain't a fair fight anymore."

After Davis' forceful shakedown, he couldn't remember the names of the officers involved and says he never filed a complaint.

"These guys, they use aliases," Davis said. "They use these Rambo names. They get people conditioned to them Rambo names, so it kind of throw everybody off. This one, he called himself 'Thirsty.'"

To Davis, there is not always malice behind the misconduct—just the incentive to meet a quota.

"They are destroying a human life," Davis said. "Take your freedom away and put you in a situation away from your children, away from your family, just for their status. For their reputation."

4.

Beyond Homan Square: US History Is Steeped in Torture[1]

Adam Hudson

The fatal shooting of unarmed Black teenager Michael Brown at the hands of white police officer Darren Wilson in Ferguson, Missouri, not only sparked a nationwide social movement challenging police brutality but also amplified media scrutiny of the US legal system. One example is the recent Guardian investigation of a detention facility in Chicago's Homan Square, where police take people for harsh, off-the-book interrogations without reading them their rights, denying access to attorneys.[2] The facility is deemed "the domestic equivalent of a CIA black site" since suspects are effectively "disappeared."[3] While this is the first time Homan Square has been discussed in the mainstream press, it hardly represents anything new or unique in Chicago, or in the United States as a whole. If anything, Homan Square reflects a norm rather than a deviation from US legal and national security policy.

Veteran Chicago activist Mariame Kaba, founder and director of Project NIA, an organization dedicated to ending youth incarceration, points out that Homan Square has long been known about but underreported in Chicago.

"I appreciate the investigative reporting by the Guardian about the Homan Square facility in the past few weeks. I want to make that clear at the outset," Kaba told Truthout in an email. "It is also important to point out that there have been allegations about Homan and other Chicago police facilities illegally detaining and torturing people for many years. In this respect, some of the local media who have characterized Homan as standard CPD practice are not wrong. People's rights in this city have been and continue to be violated on a daily basis. It has led to apathy when it should lead to an uprising."

The Guardian's report on Homan Square is quite staggering. Special police units, such as anti-gang and anti-drug forces, take witnesses or arrestees to a warehouse in Homan Square for clandestine interrogations. According to The Guardian, "Witnesses, suspects or other Chicagoans who end up inside do not appear to have a public, searchable record entered into a database indicating where they are, as happens when someone is booked at a precinct."[4] Lawyers and relatives say "there is no way" of finding out where arrestees are. "Those lawyers who have attempted to gain access to Homan Square are most often turned away, even as their clients remain in custody inside," The Guardian reports.[5] Police abuses in Homan Square include "keeping arrestees out of official booking databases"; "beating by police, resulting in head wounds"; "shackling for prolonged periods"; "denying attorneys access to the 'secure' facility"; and "holding people without legal counsel for between 12 and 24 hours, including people as young as 15."[6] The victims of these harsh police interrogations are usually poor Black and Brown Chicagoans.

However, it would be wrong to read this story and come away thinking that it's a departure from typical US jurisprudence, in the same way it would be wrong to view torture as just a post-9/11 feature of US "national security" policy. Nor is it right to view Homan Square as something unique to Chicago. Throughout its history, the United States has tortured people, and it still does, in various forms.

Torture in US History
European slaveholders inflicted massive violence on Black African slaves in order to preserve the economic system of slavery. Slavery built modern capitalism and enriched a vast network of slaveholders,

stock traders, banks and corporations.[7] Slaveholders' number one fear was slave rebellion, since that would disrupt or collapse the system. Thus, terrorizing slaves through torture and other violence was a way to control them, prevent insurrection and uphold the slave-built economic system.

Torture was inflicted on slaves in order to ensure economic productivity and docility to their masters. Slaves were required to meet production quotas; torture was deployed as a form of punishment for failing to meet those quotas.[8] Slaveholders used multiple tools to torture, particularly whipping. Whipping, for "many southwestern whites ... was a gateway form of violence that led to bizarrely creative levels of sadism," according to Edward Baptist in his book "The Half Has Never Been Told: Slavery and the Making of American Capitalism." Other torture tools were "carpenters' tools, chains, cotton presses, hackles, handsaws, hoe handles, irons for branding livestock, nails, pokers, smoothing irons, singletrees, steelyards, tongs." In fact, Baptist writes, "Every modern method of torture was used at one time or another: sexual humiliation, mutilation, electric shocks, solitary confinement in 'stress positions,' burning, even waterboarding."[9]

In addition, armed slave patrols monitored, stopped, searched, arrested and terrorized runaway, enslaved and even free Black Africans.[10] Slave patrols' main job was to punish runaway slaves and return them to their masters, but free Africans were not immune. According to Gloria J. Browne-Marshall, a professor at CUNY's John Jay College of Criminal Justice, "Free Africans were susceptible to capture by bounty hunters who could sell them into slavery. The word of a free black man in a Southern court meant nothing under the law."[11] In fact, the slave patrols' method of stopping and searching both free and enslaved Blacks can be considered a predecessor to modern-day stop-and-frisk. Those slave patrols helped lay the foundation for modern US policing. Once slavery ended, so did slave patrols, but Southern whites' fears of Blacks did not dissipate. As a result, police squads and vigilante groups like the Ku Klux Klan formed and revived slave patrols' practices.[12]

Moreover, rather than solely fighting crime, a key purpose of US policing has been social control of "dangerous classes," along with suppressing labor protests.[13] Those "dangerous classes" were usually Black people, Native Americans, the poor, the homeless and immigrants—people seen as inherently prone to violent, immoral and disorderly behavior. As Victor E. Kappeler of Eastern Kentucky University's School of Justice Studies wrote, "New England settlers appointed Indian Constables to police Native Americans," and "St. Louis police were founded to protect residents from Native Americans in that frontier city."[14] To this day, those communities remain heavily policed and criminalized.

Slavery is not the only explicit setting for torture in US history. Torture was—and remains—an instrument for furthering US imperialism. It is crucial to note that slavery and imperialism are different forms of systemic violence, with distinct roots and consequences for targeted groups of people. The roots and consequences of slavery are different for Black people than, say, the roots and consequences of Western imperialism are for peoples in Asia and Latin America. However, slavery and imperialism mutually support one another, since the US empire benefited greatly from the economic foundation built by slavery.

When the United States occupied the Philippines after the 1898 Spanish-American War, US soldiers tortured captive Filipinos, which included the use of waterboarding.[15] As part of its Phoenix program, the United States, with its partner South Vietnam, tortured and assassinated suspected Vietcong members, as well as civilians who allegedly had information on them, during the Vietnam War. US-backed death squads and right-wing militias in Latin America routinely tortured and assassinated dissidents as part of the US effort to defeat "communism" in the region.

Thus, US-perpetrated torture is not a post-9/11 phenomenon, as it has often been framed. The danger of that framing is that it not only is an erasure of history but also gives the false impression that post-9/11 torture during the war on terror constituted a unique moment in US history—an aberration that is now firmly in the past and not consistently reproduced in the present. As Carla Ferstman, director of REDRESS, a London-based human rights organization, told Truthout, "I think focusing only on counter-terrorism after September 11 gives a false picture that the US went astray and is now fixed. And I would assume that the government would be very happy with that narrative because it can clearly say that it's moved on."

Committee Against Torture

In November 2014, the United Nations Committee Against Torture released a report criticizing the US government's torture practices and other affronts to the Convention Against Torture, to which the United States is party.[16] Among those practices were the torture of detainees in CIA "black sites," lack of accountability for torturers, lack of accountability for torture committed by the US military, and numerous abuses in the US legal system, including solitary confinement and police violence against youth of color.[17]

The report also condemned the continued indefinite detention of people imprisoned at Guantánamo without charge or trial. The United States' position is that the indefinite detainees (around three dozen out of 122 total currently detained) are "enemy belligerents" who will be held "until the end of hostilities" against al-Qaeda, the Taliban and "associated forces"—that is, until the end of the war on terror, which has no defined end. This effectively makes them prisoners of war in an endless war. Criticizing that position, the committee "reiterates that indefinite detention constitutes per se a violation of the Convention." Indefinite detention also violates international human rights law, namely the International Covenant on Civil and Political Rights, which prohibits arbitrary arrest or detention.[18]

The Committee was also alarmed at the treatment of Mexican and Central American immigrants who attempt to cross the US-Mexico border and upon arrest are warehoused in US immigration detention facilities. Specifically, it expressed its concern that the United States "continues to use, under certain circumstances, a system of mandatory detention to automatically hold asylum seekers and other immigrants on arrival in prison-like detention facilities, county jails and private prisons. It is also concerned at the recent expansion of family detention with the plan to establish up to 6,350 additional detention beds for undocumented migrant families with children."

Corroborating this concern is an October 2014 report by the Guatemala Acupuncture and Medical Aid Project about the human rights violations of immigrants held in US Department of Homeland Security detention facilities in southern Arizona. The report is based on interviews with 33 adult migrants held in short-term detention from late May to late July 2014.[19]

It found numerous human rights violations in immigration detention facilities.[20] Migrant men, women and children "consistently reported" food and water deprivation. "Nearly eighty percent of adult immigrants reported being hungry when apprehended, and eighty-three percent reported being hungry when they left the custody of Border Patrol," according to the report. Another 80 percent were given "no water, insufficient amounts of water, or undrinkable water." Thirty percent of immigrants were psychologically, physically or verbally abused. Many reported sleep deprivation due to extremely cold temperatures in their cells (94 percent of adults reported this), bright lights in holding rooms, Border Patrol agents talking loudly, and "becoming over chilled due to the restriction of wearing only one layer of clothing." Immigrants were also "purposefully and routinely awoken" in the early morning hours for Border Patrol agents "to inform them of their legal options," the very time when people are least prepared to process complicated legal language and "make decisions about their legal status."

The committee also condemned the use of solitary confinement in US prisons. Solitary confinement or isolation is when prisoners are held in isolated cells with no human contact for 22 to 24 hours a day. Isolation is used to punish or discipline prisoners, but it is also used for "safety" and "health-related" reasons. (For example, prisoners who indicate they may harm themselves are often placed in solitary confinement.) According to watchdog groups like the American Civil Liberties Union (ACLU)[21] and Solitary Watch,[22] around 80,000 prisoners are held in solitary confinement in the United States, many of whom are mentally ill. Even juvenile prisoners—children—are held in solitary confinement. Time spent in solitary confinement varies, but many prisoners spend multiple years in isolation, including those incarcerated at "supermax" prisons entirely made up of solitary confinement units.

Since humans are social creatures, solitary confinement can have serious physical and psychological effects on a person.[23] Isolation can cause anxiety, depression, irritability, hostility, paranoia, psychosis, panic attacks, hypersensitivity to external stimuli, hallucinations, difficulty sleeping, violent fantasies, nightmares, dizziness, heart palpitations, self-harm and suicide, among other consequences.[24] It is for these reasons that solitary confinement is considered a human rights violation and a form of torture by international bodies and human rights groups.[25]

Additionally, the committee criticized the treatment of juveniles in the criminal justice system; life-without-parole sentences for juvenile offenders; lack of protection of prisoners against violence, including sexual assault; prisoner deaths in US custody; the way in which the death penalty is administered, along with the fact that it is administered at all; and excessive use of force and brutality by US police officers, particularly against people of color and other marginalized communities. Every 28 hours, a Black person is killed by a member of law enforcement or a vigilante, according to a Malcolm X Grassroots Movement estimate.[26] According to FBI data, a white police officer kills a Black person almost twice a week.[27]

The UN report highlighted police violence, profiling and harassment against Black and Latino youth in Chicago, following testimony by delegates from We Charge Genocide (WCG), a grassroots group in Chicago that organizes against police violence. On November 12–14, 2014, WCG sent eight young activists as delegates to Geneva, Switzerland, to present evidence of police violence in Chicago to the UN Committee Against Torture.[28] The delegates told the committee and US government representatives how police violence, harassment and profiling harm youth of color, particularly Black youth, in Chicago.[29] In addition, before the November hearing, the organization released a shadow report entitled "Police Violence Against Youth of

Color," which documented racist police violence in Chicago during the summer of 2014.[30]

More Torture and Renditions Overseas

Largely under the radar, the United States still uses torture and renditions overseas, much of it outsourced to US allies. Renditions of suspected terrorists overseas have not ceased. In November 2013, Abu Anas al-Libi was snatched by US Delta Force commandos in Libya, then detained and interrogated on a US warship without access to a lawyer.[31] He was subsequently sent to the United States to stand trial for his alleged role in the 1998 bombing of the US embassy in Kenya. Instead, he died in January at a US hospital.[32]

In 2014, the Obama administration slightly altered the Bush administration's interpretation of the Convention Against Torture's prohibition on the United States torturing and abusing prisoners in its custody.[33] The Bush administration said the treaty did not apply overseas. The Obama administration's interpretation is that "the cruelty ban applies wherever the United States exercises governmental authority," according to The New York Times.[34] This would include the US military prison at Guantánamo Bay, Cuba, as well as US ships and aircraft in international waters and airspace. However, the definition seems to exclude overseas secret prisons run by the CIA during the Bush years and US military prisons established in Iraq and Afghanistan during the wars. Those prisons were on the sovereign territory of other countries, while the Cuban government has no control over Guantánamo.

However, the Obama administration does not argue that torture is allowed overseas, because it's already prohibited by domestic laws such as the 2005 Detainee Treatment Act and the Geneva Conventions. It just doesn't want to change the treaty's "jurisdictional scope," as that, according to Charlie Savage of The New York Times, "could have unintended consequences, like increasing the risk of lawsuits by overseas detainees or making it harder to say that unrelated treaties with similar jurisdictional language did not apply in the same places."

This interpretation puts fewer constraints on US counterterrorism operations overseas.

On the other hand, while the United States' military personnel and intelligence agents are, technically, barred from torturing people, its partners are not. In November 2013, reporter Matthieu Aikins wrote a long, investigative piece in Rolling Stone about 10 Afghans who were kidnapped and tortured by US special operations forces, with Afghan interpreters at their side, in the fall of 2012.[35] Soon after his report was released, Aikins posted a video of Afghan military personnel and interpreters interrogating and torturing a prisoner as US commandos watched.[36] As shocking as the video appears, it captures a common practice. According to Aikins, "As one military intelligence soldier told me in Kandahar in 2011, they would often take a 'smoke break' when interrogating recalcitrant detainees, stepping outside and leaving the prisoner alone with Afghan police or soldiers."[37] The United States spends billions of dollars training and funding Afghan security forces[38]—and torture is routine in Afghan prisons.

Detention facilities have been transferred to Afghan control. But Aikins points out that "American military units are allowed to hold detainees for 'tactical questioning' for up to two weeks." This can often lead to US commandos abusing detainees they have little sympathy for. Moreover, while "ISAR has halted transferring detainees to some of the worst locations ... the CIA has not," according to Aikins. Moreover, Afghan President Ashraf Ghani lifted the ban on night raids,[39] in which US special operations forces burst into civilian homes at night to kill or capture suspected militants.[40] The practice was controversial and had been banned by former Afghan President Hamid Karzai in 2013, because the raids often resulted in the killing and harassing of innocent civilians. Now Afghan special forces get to conduct night raids with US commandos at their side as advisers. As conventional troops withdraw from Afghanistan, the remaining US forces will largely be special operations and CIA paramilitary working alongside Afghan security forces. They will operate mainly in the shadows and will likely continue these sorts of abuses—torture and assassination—in secret.

As investigative journalist Jeremy Scahill reported in The Nation, the CIA is using a secret prison in Somalia to interrogate suspected members of the militant group al-Shabab. The prison is "buried in the basement of Somalia's National Security Agency (NSA)," according to Scahill. "While the underground prison is officially run by the Somali NSA, US intelligence personnel pay the salaries of intelligence agents and also directly interrogate prisoners."[41]

The prison is dark and dungeon-like. It "consists of a long corridor lined with filthy small cells infested with bedbugs and mosquitoes." Prison cells are "windowless and air thick, moist and disgusting," and prisoners "are not allowed outside." Many prisoners "have developed rashes and scratch themselves incessantly. Some have been detained for a year or more. According to one former prisoner, inmates who had been there for long periods would pace around constantly, while others leaned against walls rocking."[42]

Scahill reported on the prison's existence in 2011, but such operations still continue. In fact, in a rare public admission, CIA Director John Brennan confirmed what Scahill and others have been saying about US renditions.[43] During a talk at the Council on Foreign Relations in mid-March, Brennan said, "There are places throughout the world where CIA has worked with other intelligence services and has been able to bring people into custody and engage in the debriefings of these individuals either through our liaison partners and [sic] sometimes there are joint debriefings that take place as well."[44]

When reports of torture in CIA black sites or Chicago's Homan Square come out, it is tempting to view them as anomalies in US history—momentary aberrations perpetrated by "bad apples." But they are not. They are the norm, products of the slavery and imperialism on which the United States was built. The reason why an off-the-books torture facility at Homan Square exists is because torture is deeply embedded in this country's legal and national security structures, both historically and in the present moment.

5.

"Never Again a World Without Us": The Many Tentacles of State Violence Against Black-Brown-Indigenous Communities[1]

Roberto Rodriguez

> *"They tried to bury us, but they didn't know we were seeds."*
> **–Popol Vuh**

Between my eyes, I bear a scar in the shape of a "T" that I received on March 23, 1979, on the streets of East Los Angeles. It functions as a reminder that my skull was cracked, but also, more importantly, that I did not remain silent. I won two police violence trials, after witnessing and photographing the brutal beating of a young man by perhaps a dozen sheriff's deputies.[2]

These events are seared into my memory. After coming back to consciousness amid violent threats, I was handcuffed and left face down on the cold street, bleeding profusely from my forehead. While in shock and unable to even lift my head, lying in a pool of my own blood amid flashing red and blue lights, I could see many dozens of officers giving chase and arresting everyone in sight.

This happened when I was doing research for Lowrider magazine, comparing mass violence, mass roundups and mass arrests against barrio youth in the 1970s to the violence that followed the Sleepy Lagoon murder during the Zoot Suit era of the 1940s.[3] This mass law enforcement violence against Zoot Suiters included violence against Mexicans, African-Americans and Filipino youth.[4]

One of the most notorious cases of police violence prior to the 1960s was the Bloody Christmas incident of 1951, memorialized in the 1997 movie "LA Confidential."[5] It involved the 90-minute brutal beating of seven men, all but one of them Mexican, inside the Los Angeles Police Department's central station, and one outside of his own home. Only a few of the police officers were put on trial, though none served even a year. This travesty was considered justice, an example of how the LAPD could "police its own."

Even before I worked for Lowrider, I had covered the historic trial of a sheriff's deputy, Billy Joe McIlvain, who had executed a teenager from San Gabriel named David Dominguez in 1977. At the trial, it was revealed that it was the deputy who had kidnapped and killed Dominguez, while the deputy claimed the reverse. The deputy was given a life sentence, an extreme rarity in the history of US jurisprudence, yet he served only 13 years. Nevertheless, the fact that he served those 13 years was significant because, in many cases, people who kill Mexicans serve no time at all. For example, a South Texas rancher who shot and killed an unarmed Mexican immigrant from behind in 2000 was not sentenced to any prison time at all—he was only fined $4,000, then put on probation and set free.[6]

This is the prism through which I approach the reality of police violence against communities of color—a reality that I track to 1492, and that today includes the criminalization and demonization of Black and Brown youth. Too many of us bear physical and psychological scars. Many are incarcerated due to the travesty of continual racial profiling, including beatings and killings by the police or the migra—often for simply breathing, sitting, standing, walking or driving while Black or Brown.

There is no shortage of recent examples of police violence against communities of color—violence which is primarily carried out against Black and Brown men and youth, from Michael Brown in Ferguson,

Missouri, to Eric Garner in New York City, to 12-year-old Tamir Rice in Cleveland, Ohio. Of course, it's not a new phenomenon. I remember having similar conversations in the wake of the videotaped beating of Rodney King in Los Angeles in 1992. Let it not be forgotten that the beating of King was followed, in 1996, by the nationally televised brutal beatings of Alicia Soltero and Enrique Funes Flores, who were brutalized by several Riverside County Sheriff's Department deputies after a chase.[7]

Undocumented migrants are special targets of police violence. The recent Arizona Republic investigation "Force at the Border"[8] revealed that from 2005 through March 25, 2014, immigration officers killed at least 46 people along the US-Mexican border (and they have killed seven more since). None of those officers has ever been convicted for the killings.

An egregious recent case of police violence against a migrant is that of 16-year-old Jose Antonio Elena Rodriguez, who was shot 10 times in 2012 while on the Mexican side of the border, by two Border Patrol officers on the US side. At the time, the Border Patrol issued a statement saying that one of its agents had "discharged his service firearm" after people suspected of smuggling had ignored commands to stop throwing rocks, but the Border Patrol did not specify whether it was specifically accusing Elena Rodriguez of smuggling or of throwing rocks himself.[9] These killings do not wind up in police violence statistics, because the culprits are Border Patrol or migra officers, whom labor leader Cesar Chavez used to refer to as the Gestapo of the Mexican people. These officers are accountable to no one, precisely because those they murder are primarily Mexicans.

It is difficult to compile a full list of state-sponsored violence committed against undocumented immigrants, in part because there has never been a uniform standard for accurately reporting instances of police brutality. Moreover, much of the violence committed against undocumented migrants, especially against women (including rape), largely goes unreported due to fears of deportation. Even when we set aside the particularly difficult task of compiling records of state violence against undocumented people and seek to compile a list of state-sponsored violence against Brown and Indigenous people who are US citizens, the task is still a difficult one. The FBI creates an annual list of "justifiable homicides" by US law enforcement agencies, but this list only includes incidents that the law enforcement agencies have voluntarily chosen to mention, and it excludes homicides committed by the Border Patrol entirely. In addition, any killings that the authorities deem to be "unjustifiable homicides" are by definition excluded from the list, and there is no tally of non-lethal cases of excessive force. Given the difficulty in compiling lists of state-sanctioned violence against Brown and Indigenous people, perhaps the best way to understand the relentless quality of this violence is to consider a few highlighted stories.

On January 26, 2015, Jessica Hernandez, 16, was shot to death, purportedly for striking a Denver police officer in the leg with a vehicle.[10] The month before that, on December 24, 2014, Francisco Manuel Cesena was tased to death at the Tijuana border crossing by Customs and Border Protection agents.[11] Two days earlier, a Lakota man, Allen Locke, was shot five times and killed by Rapid City, South Dakota, police officers, a day after attending a Native Lives Matter rally in Rapid City.[12] Across the country, five other native people were killed in the same two-month period,[13] while others were attacked by vigilantes.[14] Two weeks before that, a Victoria, Texas, police officer was caught on videotape unjustifiably taking down and injuring a 76-year-old man, Pete Vasquez, then tasing him twice.[15] A few days earlier—and we're still in the month of December—Rumain Brisbon was killed by Phoenix police. Two weeks prior to that, in mid-November, sheriff's deputies in East Los Angeles shot Eduardo Bermudez and Ricardo Avelar-Lara to death.[16]

At the end of October 2014, Oscar Alberto Ramirez was shot four times in the back by sheriff's deputies in Paramount, California.[17] On August 14, 2014, in Denver, the police viciously took down a seven-months-pregnant woman, Mayra Lazos-Guerrero, who was pleading with them to stop brutally beating her boyfriend.[18] A couple of months earlier, in Los Angeles, Ezell Ford was killed by the LAPD,[19] and nine days before that, Omar Abrego was beaten to death by LAPD officers in the same vicinity.[20] A few months before, in April, unarmed Richard Ramirez was executed, on camera, by a Billings, Montana, police officer, Grant Morrison, who was exonerated.[21] The previous month, Alex Nieto was killed by San Francisco police officers, riddled with more than a dozen bullets from 75 feet away by police officers dispatched to look for a man with a holstered weapon. The "weapon" was Nieto's black-and-yellow Taser, which he was required to carry for his job as a security guard.[22] The previous month, in February, five law enforcement officers in Moore, Oklahoma, beat and suffocated Luis Rodriguez to death.[23] His last words, eerily, were, "I can't breathe." And in a case similar to that of Tamir Rice, in 2013, a sheriff's deputy in Santa Rosa, California, killed 13-year-old Andy Lopez, who was carrying a toy pellet rifle.[24]

The litany of state-sanctioned attacks against Brown and Indigenous people offered thus far has not even started to touch on the extreme violence endured by the portion of our transnational community that lives across the border in Mexico and Central America. Many Brown and Indigenous people became cognizant of this reality following the October 2014 kidnapping and disappearance of 43 Indigenous teaching students from Ayotzinapa in Iguala, Guerrero, Mexico. The students appear to have been killed by the police in collusion with a drug gang.[25] In the past few years, upward of 26,000 Mexicans have been disappeared and at least 100,000 killed, caught between cartel and military violence.[26]

There has never been a time in the history of the United States in which people of color were treated by the legal system as full human beings with corresponding full human rights. Complicit in this dehumanization have been the nation's official historians (the educational system and the mainstream media), who cling to fairy tales regarding the founding of this country. These official historians often refuse to tell this country's full history, which includes genocide, land theft, slavery, state and vigilante violence (lynchings) against slaves, and violence against Blacks during the Jim Crow era. Another seldom-taught episode of US history is the widespread lynching of Mexicans from the 1840s to the 1920s, and the killings of several thousands of Mexicans by the Texas rangers on both sides of the US-Mexican border.

Mass state violence against Mexicans is not exclusive to immigration-related matters. Consider the Eastside high school walkouts, which were met by brutal LAPD violence. Memorialized in the 2006 movie "Walkout," they involved 10,000 students, who demanded bilingual education, a culturally relevant curriculum, and the end of punitive measures against students.[27] One of the founding members of the Brown Berets from East Los Angeles, Carlos Montes, related to me that the very first issue taken up by them in 1967 was the rampant issue of police violence, then the walkouts. Of note, on the other side of the country, the Puerto Rican community had rioted for three days in 1966 in Chicago, in protest over the shooting death of 20-year-old Aracelis Cruz.[28]

In those days, the Black Panthers and the Puerto Rican Young Lords formed to counter the rampant police abuse in their communities, and they supported each other.

On August 29, 1970, the National Chicano Moratorium against the Vietnam War took place, attended by some 30,000 protesters. Thousands of the rally-goers—who were also protesting endemic police abuse in the nation's barrios—were brutally attacked by riot-equipped Los Angeles sheriff's deputies and LAPD officers. This massive assault was memorialized in the documentary film "Requiem 29," directed and edited by David García. On that day, three people were killed: famed Los Angeles Times columnist Ruben Salazar along with Angel Diaz and Lyn Ward. Salazar, who had been writing about police brutality, was killed by a nine-inch, armor-piercing tear-gas projectile. No one was ever prosecuted.

Despite many hundreds of killings, only a few other cases have made such an indelible imprint in national mass media, such as Santos Rodriguez's execution in 1973 by a Dallas police officer playing Russian roulette on the 12-year-old boy's head,[29] and the 1997 shooting death of high school sophomore Esequiel Hernandez by four fully camouflaged US Marines in Redford, Texas,[30] which highlighted that the US military has been deployed on US soil since 1981, assisting in the US war on drugs and migrants.

Prison and Plea Bargains

Of course, police violence is inextricably tied to another mass form of state violence against Black and Brown people: the sprawling US prison system.

That system today has expanded to become the world's largest, filled disproportionately with Black and Brown bodies. Due to under-counts, the number of prisoners may be as high as 2.4 million, excluding immigration detentions.[31] During law enforcement encounters, on the streets and in the courtroom, this system demands silence, speedy compliance and, ultimately, complete submission: in effect, emascu-lation. Failure to be docile often becomes the rationale for officers shooting and brutalizing those they question, not to mention pinning trumped-up charges on them, which subsequently causes prison pop-ulations to swell. In the past decade, federal immigration detentions have not only skyrocketed but have accounted for at least 50 percent of all federal crimes.[32] This translates to nearly 100,000 detentions per year, often in for-profit prisons, for "crimes" that before 2000 resulted in simple deportation.

One population that the prison system almost never entraps is police themselves. One thing I learned when I worked for Low-rider is that plea bargaining, which has virtually been refined to a science, effectively guarantees that law enforcement officers never serve a day in prison. Police officers who brutalize Black and Brown people often try to protect themselves from scrutiny or reprimand by charging their victims with felonies afterward. In court, district attorneys then offer to reduce the charges against victims of brutali-ty to misdemeanors, permitting them to plead guilty and walk away with no time or time served. After the victims plead guilty rather than face the possibility of many years in prison, the officers who beat them incur virtually no risk of being brought up on charges or losing in the event of a lawsuit. Even if a victim were to emerge victorious in a lawsuit, none of the money awarded normally comes from the officers themselves.

In "Ando Sangrando," author Armando Morales pointed out that never in the history of this country has a police officer been convicted in federal court for assaulting or killing a Mexican (meaning a Spanish-speaking person) since records were started, and applicable statutes enacted, in the 1800s.

Once in a great while, "punishment" for police abuse consists of suspension or vacation with pay, while sometimes an officer gets transferred or loses his or her job—a paltry form of "justice" or accountability. Most of us who have lived or who live these realities have never equated beating back criminal charges, or dead relatives winning a lawsuit (which is extremely rare), with justice.

Young people are extremely vulnerable if law enforcement perceives them to be gang-affiliated. This criminalizing of youth has led to the use of gang injunctions and safety zones that restrict the association and mobility of suspected gang members, named and unnamed.[33] These are many of the same youth who are profiled—and, when falsely arrested, beaten or killed. In the psyche of the community, these youth are presumed guilty: they "got what was coming to them."

In 1970, the prison system in this country was perhaps one-tenth the size of what it is today. Many people attribute this immense growth to the war on drugs. But even more than that, the expansion of the prison system reflects a war being waged against people of color, against Black-Brown-Indigenous bodies—the very same colonial war brought to us by Columbus and the conquistadores. These European "civilizers" treated Black and Brown people as if their lives were worth nothing. In many parts of the country, the designated value of our lives continues to be zero.

The New and Flawed Racial Profiling Guidelines

Within the past generation, the border has become a killing field. It has become a cemetery for migrants from Mexico and Central America. And yet, in many ways, the border has extended to the entire country. Everywhere, our skin color is considered suspect. This expansion, coupled with the complicity of the mainstream media and much of civil society, means that the government can continue to act with impunity. For example, in December 2014, the US Justice

Department put forth new racial profiling guidelines that formally ban racial profiling in the United States.[34] There are, however, two huge exceptions that render these guidelines virtually meaningless for Brown peoples. Racial profiling is not banned in the "border region," which legally includes land 100 miles from the actual border, and a variety of agencies within the Department of Homeland Security are still allowed to engage in racial profiling through an expansive exception granted for "national security" activities.

Meanwhile, across the country, brutal and dehumanizing immigration enforcement raids (such as the Postville, Iowa, raid involving 1,000 agents[35]) take place, not limited to the border or ports of entry. In many instances, the officials conducting these raids function like hunter battalions. Immigration authorities hunt primarily Mexicans, but also Central Americans and Black immigrants. (According to the Black Alliance for Just Immigration, there are a half-million Black undocumented immigrants in the United States.)

As most Black and Brown youth know, it is during these racially profiled law enforcement stops that trumped-up "crimes" are committed, such as failure to disperse, resisting arrest, and of course assault and battery on law enforcement officers. Sanctioning the ability of officers to pull over anyone suspected of being an "illegal alien" is a recipe for abuse and violent escalation wherever they operate.

Historically, harassment on the streets has been the norm in this country's major cities. In New York City, it has been called "stop-and-frisk," but it exists everywhere, with or without that name. For Border Patrol, it is their raison d'être, part of their job description.

Border Patrol officers do not single out anyone who looks "Hispanic" to them. They specifically target Spanish-speaking people with indigenous features such as brown skin, brown/black hair and brown/black eyes: people who are racialized as Brown, unwanted, "enemy others." Immigration enforcement, in effect, amounts to modern-day Indian removal.

Any future immigration reform is likely to further militarize the "border." Impending reforms are also sure to at least triple the size of Operation Streamline, which today facilitates the daily conviction of hundreds of migrants in mass show trials that last an hour only, sending them to private prisons or immediate deportations.[36] According to Tucson human rights lawyer Isabel Garcia, a delegation from the Black Alliance for Just Immigration once tried to witness Operation Streamline but left in disgust because the Brown men, shackled at the ankles, wrists and waist, "all lined up on one side of the courtroom, created the imagery of Africans in slave ships."[37]

Solutions and Black-Brown-Indigenous Unity

There is a crisis of state violence directed at Black people in this country. While mainstream news agencies still present this issue in a biased and ahistorical manner, at least the conversation surrounding police abuse has been opened up due to the insurrection Black Lives Matter. It is incumbent upon those who also live similar realities to both offer critical support to this Black insurrection and speak out about state violence against their own communities.

Many from communities targeted by state violence have been working toward building much-needed Black-Brown-Indigenous coalitions. There is precedent for this. At the behest of Dr. Martin Luther King Jr., many Brown people were part of the Poor People's March of 1968. And Ron Espiritu—who has been teaching a groundbreaking Chicano/African-American Studies class for the past 7 years, at Animo South Los Angeles High School—notes that the United Farm Workers (UFW) movement itself was heavily supported by both King and members of the Student Nonviolent Coordinating Committee. In "To March for Others," Lauren Araiza chronicles how all the major Black civil rights organizations supported the struggle of the UFW. Most Native American activists of that era also joined in supporting the UFW movement.

Today, too, the silencing of Black, Brown and Indigenous peoples and the ways in which they are rendered invisible are unacceptable. The federal government, elected officials, states, municipalities and other institutions that hold power over law enforcement must be confronted. The mass media must also be confronted: We are silenced and made invisible as a direct result of where the lens is focused or where the microphones are placed. As the Zapatistas have proclaimed in their struggle: "Never again a world without us."

6.

Killing Africa[1]

William C. Anderson

In many different ways, much of the world is invested in killing Africa. At the foundation of this push is the theft of Africa's resources, which threatens Africa's subsistence—and is linked to the global oppression of members of the African diaspora, known to many in the West and around the world as Black people.

While Black people in the United States continue to battle discrimination and oppression at the hands of white supremacy, the practice of subjugating Black people transcends the borders of this young empire. Although the current (though still limited) concern for Black life has the potential to bring about some positive changes in the midst of ongoing police violence in the United States, Black life remains vulnerable across cultures and around the world.

The global attack on Black people takes many oppressive forms: disenfranchisement, forced migration, enslavement and death. The last on that list commonly takes place at the hands of the dominant society's enforcers. Those deemed worthy to protect some are also enlisted to kill the other—who just so happens to oftentimes be Black.

Frantz Fanon once wrote: "In the colonies it is the policeman and the soldier who are the official, instituted go-betweens, the spokesmen of the settler and his rule of oppression."

The police officer and the soldier are the gripping hands of the oppressor, and their work is intricately connected. This leads to an important conclusion: If we seek to dismantle the police state, we must also dismantle the military. Soldiers are the police of the world, and, like police, they are consistent perpetrators of state violence against Black life everywhere. As with domestic police forces, the active soldier's race does not matter in this regard. Even if a soldier is Black, he still serves the interest of the state and not the interests of Black people.

This remains the case when Black people become officers, or even commanders in chief. At "home" and abroad, the soldier polices in the name of imperialism, hegemony and expansion of empire. Where Black bodies are, soldiers are there to police them; they are there with the interests of protecting and procuring capital. Soldiers are required to follow orders; those orders often mean disrupting Black existence and taking Black life without pause.

The fear that many Black people in the United States experience when police are around isn't wholly unique to us. This fear runs parallel to the anxiety many Black people feel worldwide at the hands of occupying forces like the US military, their own countries' domestic police forces, and immigration patrols. A recent police killing in California illustrates many points I hope to make—both materially and symbolically—about the plight that African-descended people are facing worldwide.

On March 1, 2015, a Black person identified as Charly "Africa" Leundeu Keunang was extrajudicially killed by police officers in downtown Los Angeles.[2] A viral video of his death was circulating online before most people even had a name to identify him.[3] Africa's death is, of course, a great tragedy in itself. In addition, the video and the facts of his life suggest several important analogies of Black existence that reverberate alongside the echoes of that cadence of LAPD gun blasts.

We know these things: The police killed Africa; he was homeless; Africa was living under a stolen identity;[4] he was Cameroonian with ties to France; he was an immigrant. Allow yourself to see the montage of Black intricacies in this slaying. Many of us can relate. The collage of identities and circumstances here expresses the reality of existence for many people of African descent. The police killed Africa—and furthermore, police in their many forms are killing and will continue killing Africans globally, through both outright violence and a refusal to address the ongoing, grievous harms caused by past violence. Many current tragedies—from economic crisis to climate change to internal war—fit the latter category.

The death of the departed Africa exposes the brutal nature of our linked struggles.

The police officer and the soldier are wreaking havoc on the African continent in the service of "development," investment and military policy. Nations across the continent are experiencing rapid economic growth that does not benefit their populations as it should. Therefore, the term "emergent" has become a safe adjective to describe a continent that colonial powers, new and old, continue to try to whip into submission. "Emergence" is the notion that the interests of working-class and poor people can or will be secured along with the interests of nation-states who ultimately seek to profit off of them. Under this formulation of "development" and "emergence," building capital within a neoliberal framework will supposedly result in better lives for people suffering within an oppressed sector of society.

Helen Clark, the United Nations Development Programme (UNDP) administrator, spoke at the opening of the International Conference on the Emergence of Africa. The conference was organized by the Ivorian government and the UNDP. The World Bank and the African Development Bank also played a significant role in the event.

Clark described emergence this way: "For me, the goal of emergence is not GDP [gross domestic product] growth per se: It is the pursuit of greater human health and happiness so that each one of us can fulfill our potential and participate fully in our societies. ... By 2050, an 'emergent Africa' would have tripled Africa's share of global GDP, enabled 1.4 billion Africans to join the middle class, and reduced tenfold the number of people living in extreme poverty. These are exciting prospects."[5]

Things certainly have been "exciting" for the United Nations in Africa. In the Democratic Republic of Congo, the UN launched its first-ever UN peacekeeping force with an offensive combat mandate in 2013.[6] It also launched its first-ever unmanned aerial vehicles, or drones, in the Eastern Congo that same year.[7] The brigade served in the interests of the United Nations Organization Stabilization Mission in the Democratic Republic of the Congo (MONUSCO). An aggressive peacekeeping force might seem ironic to some, but one might say they were policing the situation.

Now revelations have come forth that the UN ignored evidence about "massive human rights violations" perpetrated by two of the generals involved in this ordeal.[8] The devastating conflict—which has left more people dead than the Jewish Holocaust—continues to rage on in one of the world's most mineral-rich regions. The people of the Democratic Republic of Congo, like many other Black people across the world, remain vulnerable to the rebel, the government and the UN "peacekeeper," who is a soldier.

This type of willful carelessness has allowed the UN to avoid major repercussions after spreading cholera to victims of the 2010 earthquake in Haiti. In 2011, 1,500 Haitian victims and their family members sued the UN in a federal court in Brooklyn in a class action lawsuit. The Guardian reported: "The UN mission hired a private contractor to ensure sanitary conditions for its force in Haiti, but the contractor was poorly managed and failed to provide adequate infrastructure at the UN camp in Mirebalais. As a result, contaminated sewerage was deposited in the Meille river, a tributary of the Artibonite, Haiti's longest and most important river."[9]

The cholera outbreak would kill thousands and infect around 7 percent of the Haitian population.[10] Ultimately, US District Judge J. Paul Oetken ruled that the UN's international charter provides it with broad legal immunity.[11] Like our police—who are supposedly here to protect the vulnerable—these "peacekeepers" are willing to dodge accountability with immunity and the protection of courts.

Why is it that the UN, like many police and military forces worldwide, is allowed to waive safety concerns when it comes to the sanctity of Black life?

To my Black eyes, watching these situations from afar, the police officer I know who "keeps the peace" has commonalities with the UN peacekeeper. Those who are given the job to "protect" us all will "protect" themselves in the name of their institutions, first and foremost. Self-preservation of the state is the primary priority.

Oppression, alienation and disenfranchisement often come in the name of protection or security. Like the deceased Africa in Los Angeles, many Black immigrants, migrants and refugees throughout the world are faced with overwhelming obstacles. These often arise at the hands of a different type of officer: immigration and customs enforcement.

Black immigrants in the United States face rampant abuses, given the intersection of their legal status and their Blackness. Undocumented Black immigrants are deported at higher rates than their non-Black immigrant counterparts while being racially profiled by law enforcement.[12] Black immigrants have faced both invisibility (when it comes to assistance and aid) and hypervisibility (to immigration officials). The face of the immigrant in the United States is often portrayed as a non-Black Latino male. In addition to facing the obstacles that all immigrants contend with, Black immigrants must also confront additional forces of state oppression that zero in on them for being Black. This trend is global: Throughout Europe, the Americas and Asia, African immigrants and refugees are tormented.

When NATO helped remove Moammar Gadhafi from his seat of power on the heels of the Arab Spring, it set off a wave of chaos in Libya. Warring militias and brigades made up of rebels and opportunists vied for power. These groups have roamed the country fighting among themselves and seeking out regional control for strategic advancement. This has been ongoing since Gadhafi's removal. One of the most heinous tragedies that has taken place in post-Gadhafi Libya is the targeting of Libya's Black residents. Many Black Libyans, refugees and migrants have routinely been rounded up, brutalized and sometimes murdered.[13] Black people in Libya have been viewed as default Gadhafi loyalists and mercenaries—causing many to flee the country. Overnight, various rebel brigades and many seedy elements were armed by the United States and used their newfound power to go about targeting Black sub-Saharan Africans.

Currently, the European Union is considering a plan to outsource Mediterranean migrant patrols to Africa. Europe has seen an unprecedented influx of Black immigrants and refugees fleeing countries like Libya because of situations like the one described above. Countries like Italy, France and Germany have debated what to do to solve the refugee crisis. Ironically, like the United States, their foreign policy and colonial histories are what created the forced migration they now hope to "solve." Refugees often end up in the hands of human traffickers and in dangerous situations like "forced rescues"—a new tactic whereby smugglers are abandoning ships full of refugees, so that the coast guard is forced to rescue the desperate passengers in a life-threatening situation.[14] The West will not change its ways to prevent situations like this: In fact, ideas like "reception centers" and "camps" are being tossed around as solutions to stop the influx.

In Israel, African immigrants and refugees have already been rounded up and put into detention camps.[15] Meanwhile, the Israeli government is preparing a new policy to deport Sudanese and Eritrean citizens who are seeking asylum. Sudanese, Eritreans and other African refugees often travel extremely dangerous distances, risking their lives across unbearable terrain, to seek asylum.[16] As I write this, Yemen is being pummeled by Saudi warplanes, causing many Yemenis to flee to Somalia as refugees.[17] Somaliland has graciously opened its ports, but other countries are not always so gracious when it is Africans who come seeking refuge. Upon arrival, the African migrant, refugee and immigrant face extreme adversarial opposition at the hands of the soldier and the police officer.

Africans can also expect to be unwelcome in more liberal Scandinavian countries (often romanticized by progressives in the US), like Norway, where public discussions about how to deport their new Eritrean residents are ongoing.[18] Inside the African continent, countries like Kenya, which have friendlier relationships with the West and growing relationships with powers like China,[19] are taking steps to keep poorer Africans out. After taking inspiration from the United States, Europe and Israel, Kenya plans on building a "great wall" to protect itself and keep out the extremist Somali group al-Shabab.

This announcement came before the recent Garissa University College attack, which killed 148 people. Keep in mind that al-Shabab is using extremist methods while partially fighting over issues of the division and occupation of land that were intensified, if not created, by colonial imposition.[20] Their terror will be mentioned repeatedly in the media, but the terror of colonialism in East Africa, which fosters the existence of groups like al-Shabab, will likely be ignored. But mentioned or not, the strong arm of oppression will continue to weigh on Africa, even on Black countries seen as "safe" to Westerners. That is, even countries with stronger relationships to powers outside of Africa—and countries that received more favor when colonialists drew up their dividing lines—are not immune to exploitation.

Certainly there are conflicts even among Black people, and we are not all one sole unanimous body. However, this does not negate the right to self-determination or give anyone the right to oppress Black people anywhere. Particularly in the United States, there is a misconception that Black people are the only group of people to express violence against one another on the planet. Of course, this is not the case: Most violence is perpetrated against people of the same race. (Most white people who are murdered in this country are killed by other white people.) Also, the reality is that anti-Blackness allows the majority of the world to see destroying the darkest people as something normal. That majority sometimes includes other Black people.

No Black person is safe—certainly not Black children. We know this all too well in the United States, following the loss of Black youth like Tamir Rice, Trayvon Martin, Mike Brown and Aiyanna Jones. A blatant state-sanctioned disregard for Black children, though not fatal, was also illustrated in January 2015 in Kenya, when police attacked a group of schoolchildren who were protesting the removal of their playground. The space where children played was being cleared so a lot could be developed. The response of police equipped with riot gear, guns and dogs provided an all-too-clear illustration that when the gas clears, it's still all about capital.[21]

The entire world knows that Africa is wealthy in resources and people. The continent could fit several of the countries that exploit it most within its millions of square miles. Land grabs, development and foreign investment are instruments that new and old colonial powers are using to continue to subjugate Africa. The price is catastrophic: With every disaster that plagues the African continent, much of the world sees opportunities to insert itself into the homeland of the African diaspora. This has been the case for some time, dating back centuries to when Arabs first came into Africa, converting indigenous populations to Islam and taking captives. Now, whether it's a Sierra Leonean woman being sold into slavery as a domestic worker in Kuwait[22] or the forced removal of peoples in Ethiopia to feed the Gulf States' and China's fervor for farmland,[23] Africa "belongs" to everyone except African people.

The current US administration has been actively exercising colonial logic by extending the US hand in Africa and throughout many Black countries since its first term. Military operations have taken place in Uganda, Nigeria, Somalia and more. Under this administration, the US has actively targeted extremist groups across the African continent and carried out activities the US public knows very little about; the United States Africa Command (AFRICOM) is specifically tasked with this. Unmanned patrols or targeted strikes are being carried out in Somalia,[24] Nigeria[25] and the Democratic Republic of Congo.

Crisis, disaster and the war on terror have all been opportunities for the US, among other nations, to expand interests throughout the larger international Black world.[26] In situations of terror and sickness, powers from the West and steadily rising East have found endless possibility. Whether it's sending troops to help "fight" Ebola[27] or battle terrorist threats,[28] every action comes at a cost.

This type of debt-based dominance is widespread and targets Black countries heavily: Colonizers still control their former colonies through the grips of the World Bank and the International Monetary Fund. Many of these countries are so indebted that they cannot break free.

Non-Black newcomers to the African continent often act in the old settler tradition. One Chinese restaurant owner in Nairobi was arrested in 2015 after establishing a "no Blacks" policy. "You never know who is al-Shabab and who isn't," said Esther Zhao, just like any colonizer looking for a reason to discriminate would.[29] Purveyors of colonialism in all its forms continue to build on the backs of Black lives; today's colonizers still view Black lives as brick and mortar.

If Black life is something that people care about, all Black life should be deemed worthy of concern, regardless of gender, sexual orientation, religion, confinement or geographic location. In the last year, I watched Black people from many different places across the planet show solidarity with one another, from South Africa to the uprisings in Ferguson, Missouri, to the favela evictions in Brazil.

An international movement to value the sanctity of Black life is needed, since the struggles are so intricately linked. In short, we are fighting many of the same battles.

For example, in 2010 a report found that the proportion of Black people who were incarcerated in the United Kingdom was seven times their proportion in the national population.[30] That disproportion exceeds even that of the US, where, despite being around 13 percent of the population, Black people make up almost 40 percent of inmates in prisons.[31] Another recent report found that more than 500 Black and "ethnic" individuals have died under unknown or suspicious circumstances while in the custody of the British police state within the past 24 years.[32] Despite this, not one official has been successfully prosecuted.[33] The former colonizer of these United States exemplifies the prison-based expression of white supremacy the United States has carried on since slavery.

Still, here in the United States, Black people are naming our dead and re-energizing against state violence. We have to name Africa. We have to name Africans. We have to name the African diaspora, because freeing Africa means freeing Black people internationally.

What is a name? Like Africa, the man whose life was taken by police in Los Angeles, many of us live homeless (even if we have shelter over our heads), with stolen identities (even if we have a driver's license in our wallets).[34] That is to say, we had our identities stolen from us, and we are alienated from our homes. You may see us as the original "misnamed"—as Maya Angelou once stated in a different context.[35] After we came here or were brought here, wherever here is, our identity did not ever come first. We don't all necessarily know where we came from, what state our countries of origin are in, or how our tribe is doing since our departure. This much can be true for the Black person whose family was forced into the West via transatlantic slavery or for the refugee who was forced to leave home to create a livable life.

Anti-Black racism is a crisis that has damaged, taken life from and infiltrated our vibrant communities the world over. The intentions of many to keep the Black world subservient, poor and over-policed—if not dead—is an all-out war. There is no reason for us to restrain our options, focus or actions to one thought process, place or culture. The African diaspora is everywhere, and we are complex. Our range of responses to anti-Blackness should mirror our existence.

From occupied West Papua to Brazil; from South Africa to Australia; from Honduras to the Black belt of Alabama; from Cuba to Mali—when our time comes, the world will see the darkest people emerge from the shadows. We will not come out of the dark; we are the dark. We are the darkest. We are Black in every shade, shape and form we come in. We have been told everywhere that we are not good enough and that everyone else is superior.

But we are all Africa. We have never been stopped, and we will never be.

7.

Say Her Name: What It Means to Center Black Women's Experiences of Police Violence[1]

Andrea J. Ritchie

Early one morning in July 2015, a new hashtag—#WhatHappened-toSandraBland—popped up on Twitter. The question pertained to the death in police custody of a 28-year-old Black woman from Naperville, Illinois, shortly after her arrest in Prairie View, Texas, on July 10, 2015.[2] Police claimed she committed suicide; her family is certain she did no such thing. They had spoken to her just hours before she was alleged to have taken her own life, discussing arrangements to post her bail.[3]

A few days later, a cop watcher's video was released by Al Jazeera.[4] You can hear Sandra Bland's voice in the background crying: "You just slammed my head to the ground! Do you not even care about that?," "I can't hear!" and "I can't even fucking feel my arm!" The video ends with Bland thanking the cop watcher for recording the incident as she is placed in a police car. Three days later she was dead.

Just over a week after the first video came out, the police department released a recording of Bland's initial traffic stop from the police cruiser's dashboard camera.[5] The video showed officers following Bland for a period of time as she drove away from Prairie View A&M

University, where she had just completed paperwork for a new job. They eventually pulled her over for failing to use a turn signal before changing lanes.

Bland calmly explained, in response to a direct question by Officer Brian Encinia, why she was irritated by the ticket she was being issued, protesting that she was pulling over to get out of the police car's way, as she assumed there was an emergency. When she finished, Encinia sarcastically asked her, "Are you done?" Bland responded that she was only answering the question she was asked, and told the officer to do what he needed to do so that she could be on her way. Instead of bringing the encounter to a close at that point, as the US Constitution—which limits the duration of traffic stops to the time reasonably necessary to investigate and issue a ticket—would require, Encinia further provoked Bland by sarcastically asking her to put out her cigarette as he finished writing the ticket. Bland asserted her right to smoke a cigarette in her own car.

At that point, Encinia escalated the interaction, ordering Bland out of her car, physically assaulting her when she asked why, and threatening to "light her up" with his Taser if she didn't comply with his shouted orders. After moving Bland out of view of the dashboard camera, Encinia roughly handcuffed her, hurting her wrists, and slammed her to the ground, striking her head and causing her to lose hearing and feeling in her arm. She was charged with assaulting a public servant, and bail was set at $5,000.

Bland was found hanging in her jail cell three days later. Authorities claim she committed suicide; her family and community suspect foul play. Facebook videos of Bland talking about the importance of taking action, speaking out and resisting police brutality contributed to the sense that Bland was punished for taking a stand for her rights.[6]

Within weeks Bland's case galvanized protests outside the jail where she died and across the nation, garnering national mainstream and independent media attention.[7] Her case is among the few involving Black women to do so since demonstrations and public debate around racial profiling and police brutality were reignited in the wake of the police killings of Eric Garner in Staten Island, New York, and Mike Brown in Ferguson, Missouri. Both media coverage and protest actions were fueled by mounting calls for a response to police violence against Black women, under the rubric #SayHerName.

The Broader Context of Police Attacks on Black Women

While what happened to Sandra Bland was extraordinary in some respects, it was commonplace in many others. A day after Bland's death, another Black woman, 18-year-old Kindra Chapman, was found dead in police custody. A total of five cases of Black women dying in police custody, including Bland and Chapman, surfaced the same month.[8] They were preceded by many more, including Sheneque Proctor,[9] Kyam Livingston[10] and Natasha McKenna.[11] The cause of death varies—apparent suicide, lack of access to necessary medical attention, violence at the hands of police officers—but ultimately, no matter the circumstances, these women's deaths are also a product of the policing practices that landed them in police custody in the first place: racial profiling, policing of poverty, and police responses to mental illness and domestic violence that frame Black women as deserving of punishment rather than protection, of neglect rather than nurturing.

Black Women's Experiences of Driving While Black

As Bland's traffic stop demonstrates, "driving while Black" is a phenomenon experienced by Black women alongside Black men. Nationally, when traffic stop data is analyzed by both race and gender, researchers find that "for both men and women there is an identical pattern of stops by race/ethnicity."[12] And in some jurisdictions, like Ferguson, Missouri, in 2013, more Black women drivers were stopped than any other group, including Black men.[13]

Bland was stopped for a traffic violation most drivers commit on a daily basis on the nation's roadways without any consequences. She was neither the first nor the last. For instance, astronaut Mae Jemison had a similar experience almost two decades earlier when she was stopped in her hometown by a Texas police officer, several years after becoming the first Black woman in space. He alleged she made an illegal turn. She countered that it was a shortcut regularly taken by almost everyone in town to get to her destination. Upon discovering that Jemison had an outstanding traffic ticket, the officer arrested and cuffed her, pushed her face down into the pavement, and forced her to remove her shoes and walk barefoot from the patrol car to the police station—a form of punishment and humiliation sometimes meted out by police officers to women of color.[14]

Sometimes, as was the case for Brandy Hamilton and Alexandria Randle, the traffic stop is followed by a search.[15] In their case, invasive and degrading vaginal cavity searches were conducted by the side of the road outside Dallas, Texas, in 2012. The officers claimed to be searching for drugs after allegedly smelling marijuana on the two women during the stop. No drugs were found. The searches were videotaped on a dashboard camera, just as Bland's stop was—and the footage is a heartbreaking show of humiliation and outrage. Hamilton and Randle were not alone. In fact, this practice was so pervasive that the Texas Legislature passed a law banning roadside cavity searches in 2015.[16]

Sometimes, instead of looking for drugs, officers conduct unlawful "gender searches" to humiliate or assign gender to transgender and gender-nonconforming people based on anatomy—as they threatened to do to Juan Evans in East Point, Georgia. Evans, an activist with the Racial Justice Action Center who has since died, turned his traffic stop ordeal into a victory, successfully leading the fight for a policy banning such practices in East Point.[17] Unfortunately, countless other instances of similar violations of transgender people go unpunished and unaddressed.

Sometimes, as in Bland's case, traffic stops are accompanied by threats and excessive force. The dashcam video of Bland's arrest is strikingly similar to another traffic stop, of another Sandra, caught on tape almost two decades earlier. In early 1996, Sandra Antor, a 26-year-old African-American nursing student from Miami, was traveling along a lonely stretch of Interstate 95 to visit friends in North Carolina when she was pulled over by an unmarked car driven by State Trooper W.H. Beckwith. Rather than approaching Antor's car with a friendly "how ya doin'" as he was previously recorded doing with white motorists, Beckwith charged out of the patrol car, gun drawn, screaming repeatedly at the top of his lungs, "Roll your window down NOW!" Approaching the car swiftly until his gun was pointed directly at Antor's head, he proceeded to violently yank the driver's side door open and tear at Antor's clothes, screaming, "Out of the damn car NOW!" Antor is heard explaining that she's having trouble getting out of the car because her seat belt is still on.

Instead of threatening to "light her up" with a Taser as Encinia did Bland, Beckwith told Antor that she was "fixing to taste liquid hell in a minute," threatening her with pepper spray. Once Antor managed to get out of the car, Beckwith threw her down on the side of the highway as cars sped by, hitting her as he handcuffed her—much as Bland was thrown to the ground by the side of the Texas road she was stopped on. Although the videotape clearly shows that Antor put up absolutely no resistance to the officer's abuse, Beckwith is heard screaming, "Quit fighting me!"—much like Encinia subsequently claimed that Bland kicked him, while the dashcam video shows no such thing.

Unlike Bland, Antor lived to tell the tale, explaining Beckwith's actions in much the same way many of us understood Encinia's: The officer was punishing a Black woman who didn't play "Mammy," who asked questions, who expressed frustration at discriminatory policing, who didn't show him the deference he felt he deserved. When asked during an interview what she believed Beckwith was thinking when he was hitting her, Antor immediately responded, "Damn Black bitch." She went on to say: "He was pissed ... Who the hell do I think I am? Don't I know where I am? This is his neck of the woods," adopting a white Southern accent for the last sentence. "That is how I interpret it." Her statement summarizes the historical context—framed by slavery and Jim Crow—of her experience, as well as the inseparable roles played by her race and gender in informing the officer's abuse. She may as well have been describing Bland's arrest, or countless other daily interactions between Black women and police that never make national news.[18]

For some women, driving while Black turns deadly, as it did for LaTanya Haggerty, who was killed during a traffic stop in Chicago in 1999;[19] Kendra James, who was killed during a traffic stop in Oregon in 2003;[20] and Malissa Williams, who was killed in Cleveland in 2015 after a police chase that also stemmed from an alleged failure to use a turn signal.[21]

Mya Hall, a Black transgender woman, took a wrong turn onto the campus of the National Security Agency just outside Baltimore, Maryland. She was shot by police as she was turning around and attempting to leave.[22] Given no benefit of the doubt, no professional courtesy and no chance to explain herself, Hall had her life taken from her as though her Black life, like so many others, didn't matter: a casualty of the presumption that transgender people of color are inherently violent and their lives inherently not valuable—and of the structural transphobic discrimination, violence and exclusion that ultimately placed Hall in police crosshairs. Hall's death came just weeks before Baltimore erupted in outrage following the death of Freddie Gray in police custody, but was not centered in the Baltimore uprising that followed.

Hidden Abuse: Sexual Harassment and Assault by Police

Traffic stops are also frequently a site of sexual harassment and abuse, as evidenced by the experiences of a dozen Black women sexually assaulted by Oklahoma City Police officer Daniel Holtzclaw, who preyed on women he pulled over, including a 57-year-old grandmother he stopped as she was heading home from a domino game in 2014. He ordered her to lift her shirt and bra, and forced her to perform oral sex on him.[23] Hundreds more such cases have been documented by researchers, leading the International Association of Chiefs of Police to issue a report[24] and the Cato Institute to conclude that sexual misconduct is the second most frequently reported form of police officer misconduct after excessive force.[25]

The New Jim Crow

A few months before Sandra Bland's death, Twitter lit up with posts tagged #McKinney. A police officer had violently assaulted a 14-year-old Black girl named Dajerria Becton in McKinney, Texas, in response to calls for removal of Black youth using a neighborhood pool.

"He grabbed me, twisted my arm on my back and shoved me in the grass and started pulling the back of my braids," Becton said. "I was telling him to get off me because my back was hurting bad."[26] Again, the officer's conduct sparked local and national outrage. Again, the case was outrageous but not unusual. Every day police officers sexually harass, tase and assault young Black girls. Becton's experience was not only reminiscent of Jim Crow–era policing of pools, beaches and lunch counters; it reflected historic and present-day patterns of gendered policing of race and borders—between communities and between countries.

Punishment Rather Than Protection

Sometimes police violence spreads into homes, in the context of calls for help. In February 2015, a Charlotte, North Carolina, police officer responding to a domestic violence call shot Janisha Fonville in front of her girlfriend, who maintains that Fonville posed no threat to the officer, who had a history of using excessive and deadly force.[27]

In the end, Fonville, Hall, Becton and Bland's cases—while each unique and egregious—are merely four cases of police violence against Black women that happened to take place in the first half of 2015. Collectively, their cases feature several of the long-standing patterns of police abuse of Black women that have played out in the shadows over the decades and centuries.

Police violence uniquely affects Black women, but not exclusively.[28] Indigenous women have been primary targets of colonial, state and police violence since 1492. Latinas like Jessie Hernandez, a 17-year-old queer Latina shot dead by Denver police in January

2015,[29] are also in the crosshairs of police profiling and brutality. Asian women are routinely profiled and subjected to discriminatory policing of prostitution-related offenses, as well as to police violence. Muslim, Arab, Middle Eastern and South Asian women have similarly endured consistent police profiling and violence, particularly in recent decades in the context of the "war on terror."

Racially Gendered Threat

The mere presence of Black, Indigenous and immigrant women is deemed unwanted, dangerous and out of place in public spaces and punished through "broken windows" policing, which echoes past enforcement of Black Codes, vagrancy laws, laws governing gender-appropriate clothing and "common nightwalker" laws. No matter how young, vulnerable or innocuous, women of color are treated by police as if they inherently present a racially gendered, sometimes sexual, threat to the peace and well-being of white America.

The truth of this assertion is borne out by the statistics documenting street stops in New York City. Although the number of documented stops of women is lower, the rates of racial disparities in stops, frisks and arrests are identical for Black and Latino men and Black and Latina women.[30] In other words, Black and Latina women are as disproportionately stopped among women as Black and Latino men are among men. It can also be seen in the 800 percent increase in incarceration rates of women since the 1980s: The vast majority of those women are Black and Latina, because drug enforcement practices and responses to poverty and violence are racially discriminatory.[31] And it manifests in the racial disparities in enforcement of prostitution-related offenses.[32]

These are but a few of the patterns that inform police violence against women of color and trans and queer people of color: pretextual traffic stops accompanied by physical and sexual violence, profiling, discriminatory targeting, unlawful and degrading searches, and the extortion of sex in the context of both the war on drugs and enforcement of prostitution laws. Punitive police responses premised on the presumption that Black women, women of color, and transgender and queer people are inherently violent and must be beaten into submission—even in the context of calls for help—are also prevalent. And the exclusion of racially gendered bodies from public spaces—and from public discourse around profiling and policing—is all too common.

Say Her Name: Visibility and Resistance

Thanks to an increasing chorus of voices, the invisibility of women and trans and queer people of color's experiences of policing is slowly lifting. The founders of the Black Lives Matter movement have notably and explicitly insisted that all Black lives matter—including those of women, trans people and queer folks.[33] Black women have also shifted public conversations through their powerful leadership on the ground in Ferguson, New York City, Baltimore, Chicago, Oakland and around the country. The publication of "Say Her Name: Resisting Police Brutality Against Black Women" also contributed to increasing visibility, as did the call for the first National Day of Action to End State Violence Against Black Women and Girls on May 21, 2015, put out by Black Youth Project 100 (BYP 100), Black Lives Matter and Ferguson Action.[34] Over 30 communities across the country responded and marked the day with vigils, direct actions and protests focused on the experiences of women like Fonville and Hall, along with countless others. Sandra Bland's death was commemorated by light actions in dozens of cities.[35] T-shirts and memes listing the names of women killed by police, along with art exhibits highlighting Black women's experiences of police and state violence, have sprung up, building momentum.[36]

The question then becomes not only whether these experiences will remain within the frame of the conversation, but also whether they will inform our thinking and action around policing and safety. It seems, despite continued resistance in some sectors and the ongoing erasure of the experiences of women and trans and queer folks of color in others, that the debate has moved past a point of no return. It is no longer tenable to continue to operate as if Black women and women of color—queer and not queer, trans and not trans—are not targets of state violence, or as if they are undeserving of attention. Of course, it is incumbent on all those concerned with police violence to take up the charge to ensure that, going forward, our analysis and actions are driven by the ways in which the policing of gender and sexuality serves the policing of race and poverty, making women, trans people and queer people of color targets of police violence in ways that are both similar to and different from the ways in which other members of their communities are targeted.

Which, in turn, raises the question of how bringing the experiences of Black women, women of color and LGBTQ people to the center of the narrative shifts the shape of resistance and the form of demands.

Take the issue of racial profiling. The conversation is incomplete unless it incorporates a discussion of the ways in which it affects women like Bland, Becton, Hall and Fonville. And remedies will be insufficient unless racial profiling bans—such as the federal End Racial Profiling Act[37]—also prohibit profiling based on gender, gender identity and sexual orientation,[38] as recommended in May 2015 by the President's Task Force on 21st Century Policing,[39] at the urging of activists across the country.[40] And policies enacted to effect such profiling bans must include measures to address gender- and sexuality-specific forms of racial and gender profiling, such as citation of the presence or possession of condoms (which are sometimes confiscated) as evidence of prostitution-related offenses or "lewd" conduct.

Centering women and trans people's experiences will also require movements against police violence to expand our analysis of state violence to include sexual assault by police, violence against pregnant and parenting women, policing of prostitution, deadly responses to domestic violence, and the routine violence and violation of police interactions with transgender and gender-nonconforming people.

It will require us to pursue solutions that are both gender-specific and inclusive: demanding that special prosecutors appointed to investigate police killings also investigate police rapes; calling for an end to Taser use against pregnant women and children; and advocating for civilian oversight bodies trained to effectively adjudicate and administer discipline in cases of sexual assault and homophobic and transphobic abuse by police.

Most importantly, it will push us beyond police reform to a radical reimagination of public safety. When we begin to understand that police are a significant source of violence against women and LGBTQ people of color—even as they are promoted as our protectors—we must question whether countering police violence is really a question of dealing with a few "bad apples" or problematic policies. Challenging police violence requires a challenge to the institutional structure itself, which is deeply rooted in policing the boundaries of race, gender, sexuality, poverty and nation. Going forward, our charge is not only to protest the killings, demand policy changes and call for accountability but also to nurture values and structures that will truly produce safety for all of us.

8.

Your Pregnancy May Subject You to Even More Law Enforcement Violence[1]

Victoria Law

As calls to end police violence swept the nation during the summer of 2014, the New York City Police Department demonstrated that pregnancy is no protection against brutality. Sandra Amezquita was five months pregnant when police threw her, belly first, onto the ground. An officer straddled her body, adding his weight to the pressure, before handcuffing and arresting her. Her offense? Trying to stop them from harassing her 17-year-old son, who had been arrested for robbery the year before.

A member of El Grito de Sunset Park, a neighborhood police watchdog group, recorded the entire event and posted it online.[2] The video sparked outcry and local protests, drawing attention to the fact that women—even women who are visibly pregnant—are not immune to police violence. That same summer, Idaho police shot and killed Jeanetta Riley, a pregnant mother of three who pulled a knife on her husband when he attempted to take her to the hospital after she had threatened suicide.[3]

But for pregnant women, law enforcement violence isn't limited to physical brutality. Police and other law enforcement frequently subject pregnant women to other, less visible forms of violence. For instance, in many precincts and jails, pregnant women are subject to inhumane practices such as shackling or the denial of food, clothing and medical care. But in many states, if a woman subjects herself and her fetus to such practices, she risks criminalization and arrest, often on charges such as child endangerment, child abuse or fetal homicide. Both the criminalization of pregnancy and the arrests of pregnant women constitute their own forms of police violence, but these are often overlooked by many of the larger organizing movements against police violence that have been sweeping the country since the deaths of Michael Brown, Eric Garner and Tamir Rice. Yet they are no less torturous and brutal than the violence being protested on the streets nationwide.

The violence that Jessica Venegas experienced was not the same physical brutality that the New York City Police Department inflicted on Sandra Amezquita. Instead, the violence and pain were inflicted by police protocol—or, in some cases, lack of protocol—as well as a lack of regard for her pregnancy and overall well-being.

In November 2011, Venegas, then 6 1/2 months pregnant, was driving when a police car cut her off. The police found 300 bags of heroin in the car, which belonged to Venegas' heroin dealer. Despite her requests to be handcuffed in front, officers placed her hands behind her back. On the ride to the precinct, she recalled being unable to hold onto anything and sliding across the vehicle. "It was really, really painful," she told Truthout.

Because of her pregnancy, police held her at the precinct rather than transporting her to central booking to await arraignment. The next morning, Venegas woke up in pain. "At first, I thought I was dope sick and morning sick," she remembered. Nonetheless, the pain was alarming enough that she told the police she needed to go to the hospital. At first, she recalled, the officers were reluctant to bring her to the hospital. "They asked me, 'Are you sure you want to go to the hospital? You're about to go see the judge.'" Venegas insisted, and so she was handcuffed, placed in a police van and driven to Elmhurst Hospital, the hospital in Queens where women held at Rikers Island, New York's island jail complex, are taken for pregnancy-related care.

At the hospital, Venegas was placed in a wheelchair with both her wrists and ankles cuffed. Doctors discovered that her blood pressure was high and the baby's heart rate was dropping. She spent the night with one hand and one foot cuffed to the hospital bed. Her feet were also shackled together. An IV was inserted into the arm cuffed to the bed.

"It was very uncomfortable," she said. "I couldn't turn. I could sit up a little, but that was it." An officer sat in the room with her. Venegas was allowed to draw the curtain for privacy so long as the curtain exposed her feet. When she had to use the bathroom, the officer detached her from the bed but left her feet shackled so that she could wobble to the bathroom and back. Then her hand and foot were cuffed to the bed again. Venegas pointed out that, at that point, she had yet to see a judge or hear the charges against her. "I wasn't technically a prisoner yet," she said. "I hadn't even been arraigned."

The following morning, Venegas noticed blood in her urine and called for a nurse. A few hours later, she went into labor and was rushed to the delivery room. Her leg shackles were removed, but her left hand remained cuffed to the bed while she was given an emergency C-section.

In the recovery room, the officer, who had left the room during her surgery, returned and shackled her legs again. According to Venegas, the nurse tried to dissuade him, arguing that the anesthesia prevented her from feeling, let alone moving, her legs. She was unsuccessful; the officer shackled Venegas.

Venegas spent several days recovering in the hospital. Her baby was placed in the intensive care unit. Venegas was not allowed to call family members to tell them her whereabouts or that she had given birth. After not seeing her daughter in court for arraignment, Venegas' mother called the precinct. Only then did she learn that her daughter had been taken to the hospital and had given birth.

After Venegas was released from the hospital, she was immediately taken to the courthouse for arraignment. The judge set bail at $10,000. Unable to afford that sum, she was sent to Rikers Island where she spent one month before appearing in court again. This time, the charges against her were dismissed.

But her ordeal was not over. Three days after Venegas was released, her daughter was placed in foster care. Although Venegas had agreed to attend outpatient drug treatment, caseworkers told her that they would not give her the baby unless she went to a residential program. Fortunately, she found a program with an open slot and, six months later, was granted custody.

Police violence—whether in the form of physical brutality or institutionally sanctioned violence—is not limited to New York City. In 2008, Juana Villegas was nine months pregnant when Tennessee police asked for her driver's license during a routine traffic stop. Villegas, who was undocumented, could not produce one. Police took her to Nashville's Davidson County Jail, where authorities learned that she was undocumented and held her under the 287(g) program allowing local police to detain people on federal immigration violations. After three days, Villegas went into labor. Officers handcuffed and ankle-cuffed her before transporting her to the hospital. She was unshackled when she gave birth, but then cuffed to the hospital bed a few hours later.[4]

"The Tip of the Iceberg"

But shackling is only one form of law enforcement violence against pregnant women. "The combination of pregnancy and being held lengthy periods pre-trial can be incredibly dangerous," said Diana Claitor, executive director of the Texas Jail Project, which advocates for improved conditions in the state's 247 county jails. Claitor told Truthout that she receives numerous complaints about jail conditions from concerned family members. In one extreme case, Nicole Guerrero was five months pregnant when she was incarcerated at the Wichita County Jail for violating probation.[5] After nine days, she noticed blood and other bodily fluids coming out of her vagina, then began experiencing contractions. A nurse told her that she was fine and had her returned to her cell, where her cries for help were ignored for hours. At 3:30 in the morning, Guerrero was taken to a different cell, where she gave birth on the floor. The baby died.[6]

"When you hear of cases like that, you realize it's only the tip of the iceberg," Claitor said, adding that Guerrero's experience is not uncommon. In 2014, Jessica De Samito, a 30-year-old Navy veteran, was jailed for violating parole. She was 24 weeks pregnant and on a methadone maintenance program. Sudden withdrawal from methadone is medically contraindicated and, for pregnant women, can cause miscarriage. The United Nations recognizes the withholding of methadone as cruel and degrading treatment. However, the Guadalupe County Jail did not offer methadone, and so De Samito reached out to National Advocates for Pregnant Women (NAPW), an organization that defends the rights of pregnant and parenting women.

NAPW filed an affidavit arguing that denying her treatment would violate her constitutional rights. NAPW also reached out to RH Reality Check, which amassed 5,000 signatures on an online petition and started a social media campaign called #JusticeforJessica. "People started calling the county jail," said Kylee Sunderlin, a Soros Justice fellow at NAPW, who took the lead on De Samito's case. The public pressure worked. After 2 1/2 days of feeling "clammy," "sick" and "incredibly terrified," De Samito was given a half dose of methadone. A few days later, the parole board announced it would not remand her to prison.

However, Sunderlin noted that the consequences extended beyond the week in jail. De Samito was released under strict surveillance with exact times in which she was allowed to go to the methadone program and in which she had to be home. For the first few days, a police officer was stationed outside her home to ensure compliance. In addition, she had lost her job during that week, in part because of the publicity necessary to secure her treatment and release, but the methadone program was not covered by Medicaid, so De Samito had to pay out of pocket for each visit. Although she found a program in a neighboring county that both accepted Medicaid and offered support services for pregnant and parenting patients, she was unable to enroll because of the inflexible hours she was allowed out of her house. Sunderlin recalled a conversation with De Samito in which her client explained, "I can continue getting methadone treatment every day or I can buy groceries." Others pitched in to buy her groceries so that she could continue getting treatment during her pregnancy. "All of this was a result of this one week of unnecessary detention," Sunderlin said.

Shackling and access to much-needed medication are two issues facing pregnant women behind bars. But these are only two examples among an array of medical concerns facing women across the country.

When Medical Care Constitutes Another Form of Violence

Tina Tinen was 41 years old, and had already suffered an ectopic pregnancy and been warned that she might never have a successful pregnancy, when she arrived at Rikers Island. She doesn't remember receiving much medical care, let alone a test to see if her pregnancy was ectopic.

"Every afternoon, around the same time, I'd get a cramp," she told Truthout. "I'd bleed a little bit." She recalled that she tried to see the doctor but gave up after sitting in the pen for hours. After three days, she asked the women around her, some of whom had been pregnant before, about the cramp. "They told me I needed to go to medical because I might be having a miscarriage," she said. The women fetched an officer and insisted that they take Tinen to the medical unit. When she arrived, medical staff told her to remove her clothes. As she did, she recalled, a drop of blood fell on the floor. "They made faces like, 'Oh shit. This one's about to drop dead.'" When staff could not find a heartbeat for the fetus, they sent her to Elmhurst Hospital. But first, jail staff shackled her. "The shackles really hurt," she said. "My ankles are really skinny and the cuffs hurt your ankles, but no one lets you wear two pairs of socks." At the hospital, the officer became angry with her for walking slowly. Hospital staff located the heartbeat and explained to Tinen that she needed to lie down, rest, and only get up if absolutely necessary. She received no follow-up care when she returned to Rikers. She was later sent to Bedford Hills Correctional Facility, the state prison that houses pregnant women, where she gave birth to a healthy baby boy.

Tinen was fortunate compared to women who had previously been on the island. In 1989, a woman experienced an ectopic pregnancy while at Rikers Island. She had not been given a pregnancy test when she arrived. A few weeks later, she began experiencing extreme lower back pain. Medical staff sent her to Elmhurst Hospital. "I was in a great deal of pain, bleeding and in shock," the woman recalled. Nonetheless, she was shackled at her wrists and ankles "while I laid there in my blood, pain and shock. This was quite horrible and I went into a panic attack. I was begging the officer not to put me in these restraints. I informed the officer that I was not a flight risk because I was due to be released within a couple of weeks. I was informed that this was basic procedure and that it was the only way that I would be transported to the hospital." There, she learned that she had an ectopic pregnancy. "The anxiety that I experienced from them shackling me was just as profound for me as the act of losing my baby," she stated.[7]

Even when medical care is regularly scheduled, the ways in which it is administered can impede having a safe and healthy pregnancy. Miyhosi was two months pregnant when she entered the jail in Middletown, New York. She was taken to prenatal visits at an outside clinic. During her first few months, she was fully shackled with handcuffs, ankle cuffs, a waist chain and a black box. After several months, she told a sergeant that the restraints caused excruciating pain not just then, but for days following. After that, she was taken to the clinic without restraints.

However, at every visit, a jail officer was stationed in the room with her. "It was hard to confide in the doctor that something was wrong," she told Truthout. "The officers repeat information to other officers [back at the jail] and then the whole world knows about it. It frightens people into not saying anything." Miyhosi had a urinary tract infection, which was diagnosed and then treated. After that, she was told that she was being tested regularly in case of another infection. When she suspected that she had another infection, and even when she was urinating blood, she did not voice her fear out loud with the officer in the room. Instead, she recalled asking at each visit:

"Can you check to make sure I don't have any infections? I have lower abdominal pain." The untreated infection affected her baby, who had to be sent to the neonatal intensive care unit a few days after birth.

Criminalizing Pregnancy: A Combination of Police and Medical Violence

Pregnancy criminalization laws have increased the number of women forced to endure these dehumanizing, violent and sometimes pregnancy-threatening conditions. Take the case of Tamara Loertscher and her first pregnancy. In 2014, unemployed and lacking health insurance, she went to the Mayo Clinic in Eau Claire, Wisconsin. There she disclosed that she had used methamphetamine and marijuana in the past but had stopped using when she suspected that she was pregnant. A urine test confirmed both that she was pregnant and that she had previously used drugs. Medical staff shared this information with social services personnel. The state began secret proceedings against Loertscher, including appointing an attorney for her fetus but not for her. She was ordered to attend drug treatment. When Loertscher refused, she was arrested and jailed under Wisconsin's Cocaine Mom Law. The law,[8] passed in 1997, allows the state to detain, arrest and incarcerate pregnant women who are accused of using alcohol or drugs, and to force them into treatment.

At the jail, because she refused to take a pregnancy test, Loertscher was placed in solitary confinement, where she spent nearly 24 hours confined to a small cell with little to no human contact. The cell contained a metal bed frame with no mattress or blankets. She was given no additional food. She spent 36 hours in isolation before she was placed in a different unit with other women. According to Sara Ainsworth, director of legal advocacy at National Advocates for Pregnant Women (NAPW), a guard threatened to tase her. Only the intervention of another guard stopped him from doing so.

In addition, she was denied medication for her hypothyroidism for the first few days, increasing her risk of miscarriage. She began to experience cramping and asked to see an OB-GYN. The jail did not allow her to do so. After 18 days, Loertscher was released on the condition that she submit to weekly drug tests at her own expense and be subjected to surveillance by child welfare. The surveillance included random unannounced visits to her house as well as access to all of her medical records. All of these forms of violence and trauma could have been avoided had the state not incarcerated her in the first place.

But Loertscher's case is no anomaly. According to Ainsworth, who acted as counsel, NAPW hears similar cases happening across the country. Quantifying them is nearly impossible. "All proceedings are in secret because they're handled by child welfare. There's no way to get information on how often or how many times this happens unless the women themselves come forward," she told Truthout. However, she does note that the increased surveillance and prosecution doesn't happen to all women equally—the hammer of these proceedings tends to fall on women of color and low-income white women like Loertscher. "We're not seeing this among middle-class white women with more resources," she said.

Ainsworth points to the case of Alicia Beltran, another woman imprisoned under Wisconsin's Cocaine Mom Law. In 2013, Beltran told medical providers that she had taken Suboxone as a way to wean herself off painkillers. When she realized that she was pregnant, she weaned herself off Suboxone. Medical providers insisted that she begin taking Suboxone again; when Beltran refused, she was arrested. Although she was 14 weeks pregnant, police forced her to kneel on the floor before cuffing both her wrists and ankles. She was brought to the jail where she spent an entire day without food or water. Like Loertscher, Beltran was not assigned a lawyer, but her fetus was.

Beltran was ordered into drug treatment for 75 days. During that time, she lost her job. The treatment facility provided no prenatal care, but fortunately Beltran's mother was allowed to drive her from the center to prenatal care two hours away. Had her mother not been willing or able to do so, Beltran would have had to go without; the program did not provide transportation.

Had anyone other than a government official inflicted these kinds of scenarios—physical restraint, the denial of medical care and no access to food or water—on Loertscher, Beltran or Venegas, they would risk criminal charges. In 38 states, violence against women that results in pregnancy loss is called fetal homicide.[9]

Indiana is one of those states. Fetal homicide in that state isn't limited to people who inflict harm on pregnant women. Women themselves can also be held criminally responsible if their actions result in miscarriage, stillbirth or infant death. In 2011, Bei Bei Shuai was 33 weeks pregnant when her boyfriend informed her that he was married and that he was leaving her. Distraught, Shuai attempted to commit suicide by eating rat poison. Friends found her and rushed her to the hospital, where she was given an emergency C-section. Her daughter died three days later, triggering charges of murder and attempted feticide. Shuai was jailed without bail for one year. Her case drew considerable media attention.

"The prevalence of suicidal ideation during pregnancy is relatively high, and, in this country, suicide has been ranked as the fifth-leading cause of death among pregnant women," wrote Dr. Vivien K. Burt, Professor Michelle Oberman and Dr. Margaret Spinelli in their brief in support of Shuai. "A punitive approach to perinatal mental illness is troubling," they continued. "Decisions about treatment for mental illness during the perinatal period are challenging to both clinicians and patients. Criminal law has no place here."[199]

Shuai eventually pled guilty to lesser charges. She was sentenced to 178 days in jail and given credit for both the 89 she actually spent at the Marion County Jail and another 89 days of "good time."[11] But Shuai now has a criminal conviction and must pay the cost of her home detention.

Purvi Patel was not as fortunate. In 2013, Patel arrived at an emergency room bleeding after an apparent miscarriage. She told hospital staff that she had miscarried but had dumped the fetal remains in the garbage. Staff contacted law enforcement, and Patel was charged with neglect of a dependent for allegedly giving birth to and abandoning a live newborn. The prosecutor also added a second charge contradictory to the first: feticide, for allegedly "knowingly terminat[ing] ... her own pregnancy by ingesting medication."[12]

Patel's conservative Hindu background, in which premarital sex is frowned upon, as well as her text messages, in which she had expressed ambivalence about her pregnancy, became part of the investigation and subsequent trial. The state presented the results of a "lung float test," a test in which lungs are placed in a container of water. If the lung floats, the test claims, it proves that the owner had breathed in air and had thus been alive. The test has been deemed unreliable for the past 100 years.[13] In addition, the state's own toxicologist admitted not finding evidence of abortifacients in Patel's system. Nonetheless, a jury found her guilty on both charges. She was sentenced to 41 years in prison.[14]

When the State Commits Violence

But what are the consequences if police, or jail or prison staff, hold a pregnant woman under similar circumstances? If Patel had suffered a miscarriage while in police custody, would they be criminally charged?

"Of course not!" Ainsworth answered. She points to the many lawsuits filed by women who have experienced pregnancy—and pregnancy loss—behind bars. "There's never been a criminal prosecution of jail staff. There may be some potential civil liability, but the criminal justice system doesn't respond to this kind of deprivation."

"It's very difficult [to hold jails responsible]," Claitor agreed. "To meet the legal standards of medical negligence, you'd have to prove that the neglect directly caused the death." In addition, she pointed out that a woman seeking legal accountability also faces the challenge of finding a law firm with enough money to hire experts. Considering that many women are held in jail because they cannot afford relatively low amounts of bail, this can be close to impossible. In contrast, local governments have numerous resources and protections to dispute any allegations of wrongdoing.

"There are no sanctions that the state will impose on its own actors," Ainsworth noted. "Traditional police violence is enabled in this setting. Pregnant women are viewed as deserving of this kind of violence. Women are brutally arrested, shackled, placed in solitary confinement and threatened with violence." But, she is quick to add, arrests can lead to violence that is less visible yet no less damaging. "The coercion to end your pregnancy or to give up your medical privacy because of the risk of having your child taken from you, all of these things basically force women's cooperation to something that they don't really consent to. This is coerced, whether you want to call it police violence or medical violence or both."

But some of the women who have experienced this violence are determined to hold local and state officials accountable for their actions. In Texas, Nicole Guerrero has filed a lawsuit against Wichita County and its sheriff, as well as the private health-care provider and the nurse who dismissed her concerns, for the death of her baby.[15] Similarly, National Advocates for Pregnant Women intends to file a lawsuit on behalf of Alicia Beltran, remains involved in Purvi Patel's appeal, and is actively seeking plaintiffs in Alabama to challenge the state's Chemical Endangerment Law.[16] It has already filed a civil rights lawsuit on behalf of Tamara Loertscher challenging Wisconsin's Cocaine Mom Law. "This law is bad for pregnant women and bad for babies," Ainsworth stated, "and it demonstrates why there should be no role for coercive, punitive state action in the provision of prenatal health care."[17]

9.

Black Parenting Matters: Raising Children in a World of Police Terror[1]

Eisa Nefertari Ulen

My child's breath is a freedom song. In. Out. In. Out. In. Out. The rhythmic pulse of air he powers is love, is life, is liberation. In. Out. In. Out. My child is breath. "I am here," his body says with each inhalation. "I am alive," his body offers with each exhalation. Each breath is a life force and each life force is a gift, is Holy. He is Divine.

He is more than mere existence. He is complex sinew, meat, blood, mind, matter, running, laughing, playing, smiling, healthy. He is boy in motion, chasing balls, jumping rivers, leaping meadows, climbing trees.

He is an idea made flesh.

He is a rebellion. A riot. A rage against the machine.

At a Black Lives Matter protest my son sounded a call: "What do we want?" He also sang the response: "Justice." The drumbeat of our fellow marchers punctuated this question: "When do we want it?" And he knew the answer: "Now." My son is The Revolution. This is why: Twelve million to 20 million African people were stolen across the Middle Passage.[2] About half did not survive the journey.[3]

From 1882 to 1968, there were 3,446 recorded lynchings of Black people in the United States.[4] That averages to about 40 people of African descent hanged, sliced, torched, drowned, beaten, or hacked each year.[5] That averages to about three to four lynchings per month, which averages to, every week or so, one Black body lynched, one Black body clawed by white mobs.

To survive this is to be a revolution, the inheritor of revolution. We are the children of those who survived. My husband, my son and I are their promise song. Because of them, we are here, and our survival is a revolutionary act.

For white people, survival is a daily experience that is taken for granted. For African-Americans, survival is a daily act of intentionality and purpose. Survival is a daily ritual Black people must perform. Survival is item number one on a daily to-do list.

I am a Black woman on a mission. I fear police violence, the merciless criminalization of brown boys. I fear the dehumanization of Black people that makes the police so swift in their use of force.

From January 1, 2015, to May 30, 2015, at least 385 people have been shot and killed by police in the United States.[6] This does not include the numbers of Americans killed while in police custody. Of the victims who were unarmed, about two-thirds were Black or Latino.

I fear more than police brutality. I also fear the lies that fuel police terror. I fear the systematic way stories about Black people's encounters with the police are twisted and turned by the voice of the state. I fear the way the narrative is controlled by the state so that even our experiences do not belong to us.

I have experienced the terror of state forces circumscribing Black life. I have witnessed the incrimination of Black people, seen the state blame them for their marginalization. We have been kicked down and then blamed for being so low. This I have seen with my own eyes.

Rodney King deserved to be beaten, Trayvon Martin was not crying for help, Walter Scott was threatening the officer, Eric Garner could breathe, could breathe, could breathe.

Cell phone cameras have offered a kind of counternarrative to these tales. And we bear witness. We do. We Black folk, we remember and tell the truth of what happened, what continues to happen, to us.

My husband and I continue to craft counternarratives to the prevailing mythologies regarding Black life. My husband and I parent our child as a counternarrative—as truth. He is brilliant, beautiful, precious, perfect. He is the embodiment of his parents' love. Our love is revolutionary, too. Every whisper I send across his brow tells him this. I tell him that we are descendants of those who chose to survive.

Our ancestors made a choice. It was a decision. As they felt the liquid parts of their own bodies seep into dust, they must have considered taking the machete to their own beating heart and slicing it. Blood is 7 percent of the human body. Water, 75 percent. Tears and sweat drip in droplets, like dew, into dust. Dust and soil and clay and loam. We are the worms turning the soil, churning earth above Earth. Drip. Drop. The self into the soil. Why not burrow underground, sleep, grow the land from the grave? Why not pour the liquid self, the essential self in? This dribble is a trick. Wouldn't the greatest trickster laugh at the sun, pound the chest to move the liquid inside, cut into the self and end this torture?

But my ancestors chose to survive. I know this, because I am here. Our charge from the ancients is transparent, explicit and plain: live.

I must ensure that my son lives. Despite the terror that is this state, he must live.

Do not reach into your pockets when stopped by police.

Do not flinch or swerve and do not ever, ever run.

When the police ask for your identification, ask them for permission to get it. Ask them for permission to reach into that exact pocket or bag before you get the very thing that they just told you to get.

Maintain your cool while all this is happening.

Politely say, "Please call my parents, and they can answer your questions."

They will continue to ask you questions. Do not answer their questions. Do not say, "Officer, I was coming from that location or going to that destination." Do not give them any information at all.

Get as much information as you can. Try to remember the officers' names, the street address or cross streets where you have been stopped. If you can, try to memorize badge numbers.

They will continue to ask you questions. Just tell them you cannot speak to them unless your parents are present.

The questions might continue. They might handcuff you and take you to a precinct. There, the questions will become an interrogation. You must only say, "I have to wait for my parents to come to me."

Your parents will come to you. We will find you. In the meantime, remain silent. Know this: We who love you are coming to you.

I do not want to instruct my son in this way. How do I free him from the shackles of psychological death, from the death of the mind, and from the shackles of emotional death, from the death of the spirit, as I free him from the oppressor looming all around?

The only antidote, really, is to give him the tools to be fully invested in his own liberation. This means showing him how to write protest banners and discussing the contributions to the freedom movement made by Ruby Bridges and Bayard Rustin, Fannie Lou Hamer and Frederick Douglass.

To enable his full investment in liberation, we also discuss his contributions to The Movement. We march with the masses in this Black Lives Matter era and show him the line he walks to move us closer to full recognition of our humanity. He is on a continuum, a path stretching through time. We pray that the same spirit that overcame the overseer will live in him and overcome the officers who act like overseers when they police Black and Brown bodies.

Enabling his full investment in liberation also means exposing him to the teachings and care of others who will not commit microaggressions, act on internalized white supremacy and undo our work. We have come this far and refuse to go back. We as a people have come so far.

I held fast to my belly the night Barack Obama became the first Black president. Our son rested there, living inside me as we danced in the streets, celebrating. Later that night, my husband and I discussed the wonder of it all, that our child's first president would be a Black man. That he would never know life without a Black president. That a Black president would be normal to him, that a white president would be a diversion from his norm. We became more intentional in our liberation parenting that night. We discussed ways we would parent to freedom.

Guiding our child to a freer way of being in the Black Lives Matter era is only the newest iteration of African-American survival. My husband and I refuse to allow anyone to dim our son's light. We refuse to allow the weight and woe of this world to wear him. We insist that he triumph. We insist on his victory. We advocate and challenge and resist. We resist racist violence. This occupation of the Black body will not be his experience.

Our ancestors stole time from their owners to teach young people how to survive. Our grandparents snatched time from their employers to teach young people how to survive. We take time to do the same. We know that saying Black Lives Matter is another way of saying Black is Beautiful. We know our beautiful Black son matters.

PART II: COMMUNITIES BUILDING RESISTANCE AND ALTERNATIVES

10.

Big Dreams and Bold Steps Toward a Police-Free Future[1]

Rachel Herzing

Police scanners, Tasers, increased data collecting and sharing, SWAT teams, gang injunctions, stop-and-frisk, "quality of life" ticketing—all of these policing reforms have been taken up to improve the quality of policing in the United States. The dominant school of thought on police reform has suggested that reforms like these make for safer communities and that improving policing will allow us to escape its violence.

This orientation toward police reform imagines that documentation, training or oversight might protect us from the harassment, intimidation, beatings, occupation and death that the state employs to maintain social control under the guise of safety. What is missing from this orientation, however, is recognition of the actual function of policing in US society: armed protection of state interests. If one sees policing for what it is—a set of practices sanctioned by the state to enforce law and maintain social control and cultural hegemony through the use of force—one may more easily recognize that perhaps the goal should not be to improve how policing functions but to reduce its role in our lives.

Today, calls for police reform in the United States are louder and more frequent than they have been for many years. Protest movements fueled by bold, dynamic resistance in Ferguson, Baltimore and other cities across the country have raised awareness about police killings, especially of Black people, and brought new voices and ideas to the fore. Those same movements are also making recommendations about policing reforms. Some recommendations have been broad and ideological, such as Ferguson Action's demand for an "end to all forms of discrimination and the full recognition of our human rights."[2] Others have involved collecting data and holding hearings, such as Ferguson Action's demand to call "a Congressional Hearing investigating the criminalization of communities of color, racial profiling, police abuses and torture by law enforcement."[3] Others, such as the Organization for Black Struggle's recommendation that police should receive "enhanced personal unarmed combat training"[4] or Campaign Zero's recommendation that body and dash cameras be required and funded,[5] are more focused on the day-to-day aspects of policing practice. And these examples are merely representative of the range of recommendations currently being circulated.

This wave of reform recommendations comes within the context of an increased public focus on police killings in the age of social media dominance and during a presidential election cycle. Context matters in determining what will be understood as viable or politically advantageous, what is perceived as legitimate, and who is accepted as having expertise. And of course the media are serving as an amplifier, turning up the volume on certain voices, recommendations and critiques, while rendering others silent.

A reform is merely a change. When people experience harms being done by the systems that govern their interactions, movements and behaviors, some of them will undoubtedly be moved to improve those systems in hopes of reducing that harm. Eager for relief, they craft plans designed to bring that relief quickly and in a way that generates as little resistance as possible. Similarly, they may recommend reforms in reaction to a set of incidents or a pattern of harm of which they are newly aware, suggesting tools or vehicles they imagine are most expedient to address that specific set of incidents or pattern. In the case of law enforcement, if the primary goal is to eliminate deaths at the hands of cops, the focus of reforms may be on the fastest way to curb those deaths by targeting the practices that most frequently lead to fatal incidents.

Making incremental changes to the systems, institutions and practices that maintain systemic oppression and differentially target marginalized communities is essential to shifting power. Taking aim at specific problems and demanding change helps build power among repressed communities in ways that are more lasting and sustainable. Without a strategic long-term vision for change, however, today's reforms may be tomorrow's tools of repression.

In the 1990s, under the influence of Police Commissioner William Bratton, the New York City Police Department (NYPD) embraced CompStat, a data tracking and analysis system used to monitor incidences of "crime and disorder" precinct by precinct. This system is meant to track, in detail, crime complaints, arrests and summonses, with corresponding locations and times. The information from all the precincts in a jurisdiction is combined and used to generate a weekly report used in management meetings among departments' leadership.

Decreasing crime and increasing officer accountability were just two of the benefits CompStat was purported to have, and it represented a reform to the previous methods for documenting daily policing practices. CompStat has spread widely among law enforcement agencies across the county and the world, and has become one of the standard tools of modern police forces. And while advocates like William Bratton maintain that CompStat is crucial in decreasing crime rates, time has shown that these rates tend to initially decrease dramatically but then increase again. Time has also led to more and more cops coming forward to describe the coercion they felt to overreport or underreport certain types of incidents to generate particular kinds of CompStat results.[6] The accountability that CompStat was supposed to encourage among individual cops was supplanted by pressure to deliver the kinds of crime statistics desired by the city's political leadership, including police chiefs and commissioners. At a time when crime rates were already falling in fairly predictable patterns across the country,[7] police had to demonstrate their effectiveness and legitimize their role by continuing to prove that they were making contact with people who would do harm to residents if not for their intervention.

In New York City, stop-and-frisk was one way that cops were able to demonstrate the power of these interventions. Before CompStat, cops had usually stopped and questioned people of whom they were suspicious and generally only searched them under reasonable suspicion of danger (usually involving suspicion of carrying a weapon). The broken windows orientation underlying Bratton's mode of policing, which also extended to CompStat, suggested that the very presence of suspicious persons was a danger to the community. Through CompStat, the police could demonstrate that they were neutralizing that danger.

Soon, "stop and question" transitioned to "stop and question and frisk," and eventually to stop-and-frisk. By 2011, the NYPD was doing over 684,000 street stops per year, nearly 90 percent of which resulted in no arrest or summons.[8] These stops disproportionately targeted people of color (especially Black people), young people, homeless people, and queer and trans people. The depth and breadth of the physical and psychological harm done by the practice of stop-and-frisk ignited a citywide campaign to eliminate the practice and resulted in a lawsuit against the city based on the practice's racial bias. While CompStat is still prized by departments across the country, the longer it is used, the more clearly the problems inherent in its use become evident.

The specialization of policing is another reform meant to reflect responsiveness to the changing needs of police forces and the residents they police. As modern policing has evolved, many forces created units to focus on specific areas of crime such as homicide, gangs or vice. One of the most notorious of these units is Special Weapons And Tactics (SWAT) teams.

First used in the mid-1960s as small, elite units designed to respond to situations requiring paramilitary force and precision, SWAT and other paramilitary policing units have ceased to be the exception in policing and have become the rule. Roughly 90 percent of all police departments in cities with populations over 50,000 have some type of SWAT team,[9] as do federal departments including the Department of

Agriculture and the Department of Education. Additionally, SWAT teams routinely run training for new cops. They are used in a wide range of policing activities, from traffic stops to seeking informants to more high-impact policing. And although SWAT is a reform initiated from within law enforcement, its overwhelming expansion and mission creep are consistent with other forms of police specialization.

Keeping the function of policing in focus—armed protection of state interests—increases clarity about what policing is meant to protect and whom it serves. Further, that clarity helps us reflect on what asking for police accountability really means. Police forces tend to be very accountable to the interests they were designed to serve, and those interests frequently clash with the interests of the communities targeted most aggressively by policing. Recognizing policing as a set of practices used by the state to enforce law and maintain social control and cultural hegemony through the use of force reveals the need for incremental changes that lead toward the erosion of policing power rather than its reinforcement. This recognition may also move us toward ways to reduce the impacts of the violence of policing without ignoring the serious issues that lead to violence within our communities.

For anyone with experience dealing with the grinding harassment, psychological or physical harm, or death meted out by policing, it's clear that the best way to reduce the violence of policing is to reduce contact with cops. Plans for change must include taking incremental steps with an eye toward making the cops obsolete, even if not in our own lifetimes. Taking incremental steps toward the abolition of policing is even more about what must be built than what must be eliminated. Further, it requires steps that build on each other and continue to clear the path for larger future steps while being mindful not to build something today that will need to be torn down later on the path toward the long-term goal.

The context created by the powerful protest movements referenced above has created an opportunity to make bigger, bolder changes than we have seen in a very long time. Now should be the time to draw from the organizations that have been hard at work making that change on the ground and to test out creative new approaches built on community experience, rather than attempting to develop brand-new government-driven strategies, repackage reforms already in the Department of Justice pipeline, or reintroduce old reforms such as civilian review boards that have a demonstrated track record of being more theater than substance.

Here are just a few examples of ideas that have received less attention than body cameras or special prosecutors, but are promising incremental steps toward eroding the place and power of policing in US communities: Youth Justice Coalition's 1% Campaign advocates for just 1 percent (roughly $100 million) to be diverted from the Los Angeles Police Department budget and directed toward programs and services for young people that are alternatives to youth suppression.[10] Similarly, Los Angeles Community Action Network's (LA CAN) Share the Wealth Campaign advocates for investments to be more equitably distributed in Los Angeles' Downtown neighborhood, so that they benefit all residents without displacement or fear from police violence.[11] Given adequate resources and the opportunity to develop, imagine what such incremental shifts of funding priorities could create.

Projects such as the Harm Free Zone project in Durham, North Carolina,[12] and the Audre Lorde Project's Safe OUTside the System Safe Neighborhood Campaign[13] are testing grounds for community responses to harm that do not rely on law enforcement interventions. The Harm Free Zone is building community knowledge and power to enable community members rather than the police to be called upon as first responders. The project educates and trains interested Durham residents to intervene in situations of harm without police intervention. Based in Brooklyn, New York, the Safe Neighborhood Campaign focuses on reducing harm to lesbian, gay, bisexual, two-spirit, trans and gender-nonconforming people of color by working with local businesses and community spaces to provide safe haven for people in need without contacting the police. The campaign also trains campaign partners on combating homophobia and transphobia and developing strategies for addressing violence without calling the police.

These projects have been replicated in cities across the country and could serve as models in scaling up these kinds of community-based interventions. Meanwhile, the StoryTelling & Organizing Project[14] reminds us that people are already using creative means to address interpersonal harms every day, without police intervention. These projects take seriously the harms that generate fear, violence and even death, but also understand that police intervention is not the right remedy.

Broader-reaching ideas, such as eliminating the use of police forces in addressing mental health crises instead of creating special teams of mental health cops (see Chapter 15), ending the use of broken windows policing,[15] or banning cops who use excessive force from any employment in any type of law enforcement (public or private), are just some of the bolder recommendations currently being circulated.

This is the era for bold ideas and big dreams. While "the whole world is watching," monitoring how the United States will address its policing crisis, why not take steps forward instead of backward? Why not move toward a future free of the violence of policing, rather than one that has merely improved the efficiency of its killing machine? The surest path toward a freer, safer future is one that aims to eliminate contact between violent police forces and the people they target. Why not start taking steps down that path today?

11.

We Charge Genocide: The Emergence of a Movement[1]

Asha Rosa, Monica Trinidad and Page May

Dominique Franklin Jr. was killed by Chicago police in May 2014. He was 23 years old and Black. He was loved, and people called him Damo.

Following his death, a group of Damo's friends, friends of his friends, and local Chicago activists came together. In the room were young poets of color, longtime local organizers, lawyers and others, all coming from differing vantage points but connected by their opposition to the oppressive system of policing and prisons. In the context of a Black person being killed by police every 28 hours,[2] our project was to declare that there is nothing normal about a system in which racist death and violence is routine and to prove that we will not treat it as such.

With young organizers of color at the forefront and mentors to ground us, we decided to create a new project: a reiteration of the effort of a group of Black activists who in 1951 took a petition to the United Nations. The petition, called "We Charge Genocide," cited over 150 police killings of Black people in the United States. We decided to compile a similar report about police violence against youth of color in Chicago and to send a delegation to Switzerland to present the report to the UN Committee Against Torture.

Using the name We Charge Genocide[3] and centering Damo's story in our work, we rooted our undertaking in the connections between history and our contemporary realities. Our adopted name recalled parallel tactics from a moment in time when conversations about anti-Black violence were being brought to a world stage, specifically in relation to anti-colonial movements in Africa, and there was a more broad-based political coalition for global and diasporic Black solidarity.

A member of our group, Ethan Viets-VanLear, created the video "For Damo" to tell Damo's story, summarizing the circumstances surrounding his killing and using a spoken word piece to offer a eulogy for Damo and also to indict the structures and institutions that contributed to his death.[4]

Mariame Kaba, an organizer and educator based in Chicago at the time of the emergence of our group, described it this way: "Out of the despair of his friends, a social and political quilt to resist racist policing was created. Damo's friends and peers traveled to Geneva to charge the US with genocide."[5]

Delivering Our Petition to the UN

There's a long legacy of organizers, revolutionaries and leaders taking their stories and struggles to the United Nations. Our decision to bring our report there was not a unique one; it was knowingly built upon the work of those before us.

By grounding and naming ourselves with that history, we contextualized our struggle against police violence. This history not only gave us more momentum but also helped prepare us for pushback. We learned about the repression and harassment William L. Patterson received as he attempted to deliver the original "We Charge Genocide" petition to the United Nations in the 1950s. We saw how Paul Robeson was completely blacklisted from history books for telling the world about the genocide of Black people in the United States. It was critical to build upon an acknowledgment of this history in our efforts to end the unremitting war on Black people.

While the idea of taking our report on police violence against Black and Brown youth in Chicago to the United Nations was not new, sending eight young people of color to share this report was. Eight young artists, poets, organizers, leaders and activists of color made up our unique delegation, which would tell the world what the Chicago Police Department did to Dominique Franklin Jr.

We knew going into the trip that delivering this report to the United Nations was not our end goal. Our expectations for any substantial results as far as accountability measures being implemented in Chicago as a result of this trip were very low. The power of this trip to the United Nations was not held in the formalities. It was not held in the system. It was not held in the two minutes allotted to us to speak on an entire community's destruction at the hands of the state. We brought the power with us to the table. We brought personal narrative to a space that is often overpowered by data and cold numbers. We brought a delegation of young people of color, many of whom have experienced police violence firsthand, into a space of representatives and advocates. We brought truth. We brought powerful narrative. We brought unconventional action.

We made connections with other groups testifying about police violence in their own cities. We made a very public and critical connection between the repressions our Black and Brown communities face every single day and the ways the state uses violence to maintain that repression.

We took this to the United Nations because we wanted to amplify the incredible work that young people of color are already doing in Chicago to challenge and interrupt police violence and impunity.

We took our petition to the United Nations because it was what we had to do after the police killed Damo. Mariame Kaba captured this truth in her Prison Culture post "To Damo, With Our Love ...": "So much of what we do in the name of the dead is really for us the living. It's so we can try to make sense of the senseless. It's so we can carry on and move through our grief. It's so we don't follow the dead into their graves. ... They (we) have done all of this in Damo's name. ... We struggle out of profound love. It's a love that sustains and strengthens us. It's a love that convinces us that we will eventually win."[6]

Our Debt to the Dead

How do we honor our debt to the dead?

Every new name we are forced to swallow—not to mention those who are killed by police but never make the headlines or appear in our social media timelines—adds unbearable weight to the responsibility. The reformist pathways suggested by the current "justice" systems offer little hope of rest: They are merely old logics, wrapped up in new politically correct rhetoric and fancy technology.

Police violence is and always has been state-sanctioned violence. We must understand police violence to be rooted in historical and systemic anti-Blackness that seeks to control, contain and repress Black bodies through acts of repeated violence. As our delegation stated during our two-minute testimony before the US government during the civil society consultation in Geneva:

> There is no legitimate mechanism for pointing to the police as source of violence, and what that tells us is that violating our bodies does not count, that our safety does not matter. This narrative goes back to enslavement of Black people in the US, a history of Black Codes—laws that rendered Black people criminal for doing anything and nothing at all, to the state-sanctioned lynching and rape of Black bodies as spectacle and as sport.
>
> ... The US legal system has since functioned to uphold hierarchies and justify criminalization, police and punishment. ... We are in a perpetual state of crisis that cannot be fixed from within the system. We need a rethinking of how safety can be achieved. We need power to be shifted from y'all's police to our people.

Our struggle for justice demands much more than any single indictment. It cannot be litigated, legislated or bought into existence. And there is no amount of money that could make up for the lives and human dignity lost to police and state violence against our communities. Instead, if we are to truly honor the magnitude of the injustice, we must commit ourselves to nothing less than the complete transformation of society.

We owe it to Damo to imagine a world beyond police and prisons. What happened to him reveals the true function of the police: to serve and protect the interests of property.

We owe it to ourselves to build a world in which we all get to be whole. This requires us to center the leadership of those most affected by state violence: those of us who have been deemed undesirable, disposable or inferior. Only by centering those at the margins (of race, gender, sexual orientation, class and ability) can we actually dismantle and transform our social relationships and institutions to be radically inclusive.

We owe it to all of us, lost and living, to engage in the ongoing struggle to transform the world, ourselves and our relationships to each other.

Rest in power, Damo. May you know you are remembered. Out of your life and death, revolution is growing.

12.

Heeding the Call: Black Women Fighting for Black Lives That Matter[1]

Thandisizwe Chimurenga

The year 2015 began much like 2014 ended. Since August, the United States has seen a resurgence of direct action and civil disobedience reminiscent of the civil rights movement of the 1960s. This latest wave has been a response to the extrajudicial murders of Black people by police—young Black males in particular—and the seeming inability of the justice system to hold their murderers accountable. And it has been headed largely by Black women activists and organizers.

More militant and sustained than the Occupy protests of a few years ago, or the World Trade Organization protests during the latter part of the 20th century, this movement, which began in Ferguson, Missouri, and has traveled worldwide, has been just as dedicated to affirming the value of Black life as it has been to condemning state-sanctioned violence against Black bodies.

While Black women are also victims of murder by police, the tally is not as high as for Black men. And, while many of their names are known and the circumstances of many of their deaths are similar to the murders of Black men, the level of outrage and protest has not been comparable. The reasons for this are varied.

Black women's motivations for intimate involvement in this movement, however, appear not to be as varied. Several activists and organizers behind the Black Lives Matter protests and in solidarity with Ferguson expressed a similar set of motivations for their participation to Truthout. They said they became involved because they felt they "had to."

"As a mother, I was concerned for the future of my children and my community, so I felt compelled," said Melina Abdullah, a university professor of Pan-African Studies and an organizer with Black Lives Matter–Los Angeles. "I didn't feel like it was a choice. It was a duty."

Ash-Lee Woodard Henderson, a Chattanooga, Tennessee, organizer with Black Lives Matter, concurred. "I got involved in this movement because I felt required to fight for the lives of myself and my loved ones," she said.

Cat Brooks, who works with the BlackOut Collective in West Oakland, sees her involvement as her life's work. "This is what I'm called to do," she said. "I don't know how to do anything else."

UCLA graduate student Shamell Bell said she had a "visceral reaction" to imagining her son victimized by the same state violence and anti-Black racism that killed Eric Garner and Michael Brown. "I simply could not theorize about systems of inequality as a student of African-American history and not put it to praxis," she said.

Jasmine Richards, a lobbyist in Pasadena, says she joined the movement to affirm the value of Black lives, but not solely because they were being victimized by police. "The reason why I felt compelled to do this work is because my friends keep dying. Black on Black violence, Brown on Black violence, they keep getting murdered, and I'm tired of putting their faces on T-shirts, or tattooing their name on me somewhere. I'm tired of it," Richards said.

From a "Moment" to a "Movement"

Many of the people Truthout spoke with also have in common the view that what is currently happening is a movement, not a flash-in-the-pan event or a fad, which has also fueled their involvement.

"My generation has been waiting for a moment like this, where the whole world seems to wake up all at the same time and pay attention to what we've been screaming for as long as we've had breath," said Cat Brooks.

Mary Hooks, an organizer with Southerners on New Ground (SONG) in Atlanta, agreed. "I think August 9 [the day Michael Brown was killed] changed everybody," Hooks said. "The world was on fire; our consciousness was open; kind of like [what happened] during Trayvon Martin. People were on high alert and in the streets, people wanted to make changes; so as an organizer, I look for that moment where we can provide an opening, an entry point, for people to do the work and find their own liberation."

"I have always said I wished I was coming of age during the civil rights movement because I wanted to be a part of change," said Shamell Bell. Bell was a part of Justice for Trayvon Martin–Los Angeles, the predecessor to the Los Angeles chapter of Black Lives Matter. "I knew it was my chance to do work in a movement as I have always imagined was my purpose and my vision."

"People keep narrowing it and it's so much more," said Jasmine Richards. "I see [Black Lives Matter] as a statement that gave life to a place that didn't have life. It's opening up a whole new world to a lot of us. It's making us love each other and it makes us speak to one another: ask how we're doing instead of 'mean-mugging' or 'mad-dogging' one another," Richards said.

No More Business as Usual

Activists in Ferguson, Missouri, have been conducting the longest sustained protest against police violence in the history of the United States, continuously demonstrating since August 10, 2014. Their tactics have also been creative. In addition to "protest favorites," such as police stations, courts and City Hall, activists have also made operagoers and St. Louis Rams fans take note of the injustice in the Michael Brown case. The determination and creativity of Ferguson protesters have created the template for organizers elsewhere.

In Los Angeles, Black Lives Matter's predecessor, Justice for Trayvon Martin–Los Angeles, took protests over the acquittal of George Zimmerman in the summer of 2013 to Beverly Hills' glitzy and glamorous Rodeo Drive. Since the refusal of grand juries to indict Darren Wilson and Daniel Pantaleo for the murders of Brown and Garner, they've disrupted Christmas shoppers at The Grove on the city's West Side, shut down a portion of the busy Hollywood Freeway, and occupied the Los Angeles Police Department's headquarters for 18 days to bring attention to the killing of another unarmed Black man, Ezell Ford, around the same time as Brown was killed in Ferguson.

"These state-sanctioned murders have taken place with limited impact on non-Black people, while at the same time, they are destroying Black communities," said Abdullah, "so we wanted to say that this kind of violence can't exist in our communities and be meted out to our people without the disruption of white supremacist patriarchal capitalism."

Actions in the San Francisco Bay Area—a shutdown of some Bay Area Rapid Transit (BART) trains on "Black Friday," the padlocking of the Oakland Police Department (OPD) headquarters, a "wake-up call" on the front lawn of Oakland Mayor Libby Schaaf, and "Black Brunch"—have been organized with the same principle in mind, according to Brooks and Brianna Gipson.

"[It's about] inserting ourselves into spaces where we are not normally present or welcome, and, if we are present, we are silenced in a variety of ways," said Gipson, a San Francisco paralegal and organizer of "Black Brunch," which brings the issue of state-sanctioned violence directly into eateries and cafes. "We [also] went to a furniture store in Hayes Valley ... called 'Plantation.' ... We needed to be in there," Gipson said.

"BART was chosen specifically because of their role and very long history of egregious crimes against the Black community; OPD is the perpetrator of the crimes that are part of the state's war against Black people, and so why not take the resistance directly to their doorstep?" Brooks said.

"The mayor, Ms. Schaaf, has a horrific history when dealing with police terror in Oakland," Brooks added. "From her support of the Urban Shield Conference (showcasing military-grade weapons and technology), to the handling of the Alan Blueford murder, to announcing on her first day in office that the police were her most important priority—not the hungry, not the homeless, not education, not jobs—she actually told us that the police ... were her most important priorities ... so it became clear to us that we needed to communicate to Ms. Schaaf that actually, the people are going to be her priority while she is mayor of Oakland."

"My family stopped going to the Rose Parade when I was about 7 or 8; we just felt there was no place for us here," remembers Jasmine Richards. "And so with all the things occurring in the world with young Black folks, with our lives disregarded, I felt it would be important to do a demonstration [there], especially with the first Black Rose Parade queen ever, in history. They needed to know it would be no more business as usual," Richards said.

When they say there is "no more business as usual," the activists aren't just talking about what they feel is an indifferent (white) public.

In Erika Totten's view, it's also about the character of the protests themselves. That was made abundantly clear to the Rev. Al Sharpton of the National Action Network when he called for a national protest against police brutality in August in Washington, DC. Totten took to the stage during the event and physically took the microphone from the moderator, demanding that Ferguson activists, who were not on the program to speak, be given time to address the audience.

"We said if there were no young people from Ferguson [many of them were present in DC at the time] speaking, we're shutting it down. He should have known that's what we do: We shut it down," said Totten. "If he had contacted us and talked to us, we would have told him that what he is doing is problematic; we're not doing symbolic marches anymore."

Totten also criticized Sharpton for what she called the erasure of Black female victims of police murder. "We also would have told him that there are no families of women who have been murdered by police [on the stage with him]. There are so many women who are erased because he uses the families that are national news, and that's problematic."

The Washington, DC, metro area has been a prime location for protests by Totten and other activists. Totten, a spiritual life coach and stay-at-home mom based in Alexandria, Virginia, and her comrades have shut down the I-395 freeway that runs through the DC-Maryland-Virginia area, as well as various metro rail lines and the area surrounding Pentagon City. They have also held die-ins at the Department of Justice and joined with others who called for a job walkout in the city of DC.

Where Is the Movement Headed?

Oprah Winfrey has expressed her concerns that the current phase of activism appears to be leaderless and lacking in clear demands.[2] Social media recorded a backlash of sorts against the media mogul, stressing that the leadership and coordination are present and accounted for, despite what Winfrey may think she has observed.

According to Ash-Lee Henderson, "We're creating multitiered strategies with a diversity of tactics, including direct action and civil disobedience. ... Our movement is dynamic, and we are learning from and with each other how to do this work effectively, every day. Developing more and more leaders and organizers and activists, and we're not going to stop."

As Ferguson activist and rapper Tef Poe put it, "This is not your grandparents' civil rights movement."

That being the case, where do the activists and organizers in the forefront of the movement see it headed? Again, their replies were strikingly similar.

"There is a short term and a long term," said Melina Abdullah. "We have to think about the ways that state-sanctioned violence against Black people is tied to a system that keeps us oppressed, so really what we are talking about is a complete transformation of the existing system."

Cat Brooks agreed and added that the rebuilding of society must be one "where Black women, men and children are clear that their history did not begin in the Middle Passage, and are fully aware of the beautiful beings that they are, and as a result of that awareness have a deep love for themselves and their brothers and sisters."

"We are in a wartime right now, and 'Black lives mattering' and justice is the building of the practice of reaching our destiny," said Jas Wade, who self-describes as "a Black genderqueer being of Afrikan descent." "There is a tradition of fighting and strategy and autonomy, and I want to stress the destiny aspect. We are such a resilient people; [we are] connected to the tradition of revolution, Haiti, the Maroons."

For Mary Hooks, Black people being self-determining, building on a legacy of resistance and continuing to fight for justice are as important as practical concerns. "It looks like being able to have safety and dignity, me being able to raise my 2-year-old in a community where she is valued and her well-being is as important to me as it is to the people around her we pay to make sure she is safe and educated."

Like the others, Hooks acknowledges that it will take time to fully realize the vision where "Black women, queer, trans, poor and otherwise marginalized Black folks are free to be their fullest selves in our communities and movement spaces and everywhere." Like Melina Abdullah, she sees a short term and a long term. Hooks thinks that both observers and participants should be patient with the process.

"Actions may seem like they are not doing anything, but it is an opportunity for folks to contribute to this movement and bring them closer to this work, people who have never used the word 'justice' before," Hooks said.

"Keep watching. This is the year of 'resilience and resistance.' Keep watching."

13.

Our History and Our Dreams: Building Black and Native Solidarity[1]

Kelly Hayes

As the movement for Black Lives enters its second year, some non-Black activists, like myself, have been moved to think critically about the intersections of struggles within the Black community and the struggles of our own peoples. As an Indigenous activist, I am moved by the knowledge that the same structures that have long maintained both Black and Native disposability continue to crush our young people and brutalize our communities. But despite these intersections, our efforts to build forward together have at times fallen into crisis, and the work of reconciling our differences has often been left undone.

In 2014 and 2015, from Baltimore to Oakland, Indigenous activists have come out in support of Black lives. While there have been some moments of disagreement, many Native people have successfully adopted supportive roles in the Black Lives Matter movement. While Indigenous people are killed at a higher rate by police than any other racial group in the United States—as highlighted by the recent cases of Paul Castaway and Sarah Lee Circle Bear—many Native activists see the value of investing our efforts in a movement for Black liberation and survival. Both of our communities live in the shadow of genocide and historical trauma, and many of us believe that neither of our communities can be free without the liberation of the other.

Some organizers, both Black and Native, firmly believe that building forward at the intersections of our movements could lead to the development of a new praxis, one that could bring the kind of liberation that many are only now learning to imagine, but such efforts involve a number of complex stumbling blocks.

A Complicated History

As the child of a father who had been removed from the Menominee Reservation prior to the American Indian Child Welfare Act,[2] I could easily have drifted through my young life without any connection to Native culture beyond the Mystical-Indian narratives prevalent in modern film and television. Fortunately, my family connected with a member of our tribe who was deeply rooted in our culture. Esther, who in time became a full-fledged medicine woman, taught my sister and me tribal dances and told us stories from her time with the American Indian Movement (AIM). Through her heartbreaking tales of resisting the forced sterilization of our women and displacement of our children, I experienced the first stirrings of my radical imagination.

In my teenage years, I read more deeply into the history of AIM, including the 1973 siege at Wounded Knee. As hundreds of Oglala Lakota and AIM supporters occupied the town of Wounded Knee, South Dakota, in protest of corruption and in defense of their own lives, law enforcement responded with militarized force. Armored personnel carriers, grenade launchers and other tools of war were brought to the boundaries of the siege. While media coverage was heavy, and public sympathy for the Indigenous activists was uncharacteristically high, activists feared that coverage of other major news stories would soon eclipse their struggle, and that law enforcement would roll through the town, inflicting violence indiscriminately.

The legacy of the land the resisters were occupying encapsulated both their historical grievances and their fears of looming reprisal. During the original Wounded Knee massacre of 1890, government soldiers on horseback rode down men, women and children. Infants and the elderly alike fell dead in the snow as a people's collective hope was punished by the state. The massacre was an effort to stomp out the Ghost Dance movement, which was a Native cultural and spiritual movement that had spread through most of the western United States near the end of the 19th century. The ghost dancers believed that a transformation was possible, and that a spiritual rebirth and return to the old ways would bring back the buffalo and repel the colonizers. The US government had no regard for Native spiritualism, but it no doubt recognized the danger of an oppressed people investing themselves in a belief that their salvation was possible.

So nearly a century later, AIM held the Knee and waited each day for the public's attention to fade, and for the stand-off's violence to intensify.

Amid my readings on these events, I eventually came across a story that I had never heard before and have rarely heard discussed in the years since. Angela Davis, the Black freedom fighter and scholar who authored "Are Prisons Obsolete?," actually traveled to the boundaries of the siege and attempted to join the Wounded Knee protesters. She was turned away by law enforcement at the town's border as an "undesirable" person.[3]

As I read of her attempt to join the resisters, I thought that Davis had to have known such a response from law enforcement was likely. She was already well-known and well-respected for her radical beliefs and aspirations, and was definitely viewed as a threat by the power structure. Then I thought about the threat of waning media attention, and it occurred to me: Showing up, by itself, was a defensive act. Davis used her prominence to create a news story, and for those living in struggle within the siege, visibility was life.

While most of us are not renowned radical voices and cannot offer such a spotlight by showing up for our natural allies, Davis' appearance at the siege imparted something to me. In moments of great significance, we have to bring what we can, and do what we can, because the same structures have always been at war with both Black and Native bodies.

Black bodies have always been abused, controlled and subject to social death in order to facilitate their commodification. Even the 13th Amendment provided a loophole in the abolition of slavery, allowing the practice to continue within the US prison system. Thus, the Black Codes and the prison-industrial complex have allowed slavery to reinvent itself across the course of US history, just as displacement, forced relocation, the toxification of land, forced sterilization, and the intentional maintenance of poverty have allowed the government to continue to pursue its primary goal with regard to Native bodies: our total annihilation. Social, physical and political subjugation have always been the norm for both Black and Native peoples under this government. While the mechanisms of our respective genocides have always had different aims, both have been enforced by the same structures for the sake of colonial dominance, with horrific consequences.

Throughout its development as a young empire, the United States has needed a narrative to propel its ascension. In order to create the idea of "America," a great country with inherently great people, a national identity needed to be manufactured, and "Americans" had to be created. Assimilation has always been a path to privilege in the United States. American nationalism fashions a glorious identity for those who accept the erosion of their heritage and embrace the shared plainness of the most elite identity our country has to offer—that of the white American.

The idea of America was a bright and shining lie, and a very appealing one, but the architects of that lie encountered a number of impediments. There were human obstructions, for example, whose annihilation had to be woven into a cultural identity that celebrated the idea that all men were created equal. Thus, a narrative of righteous conquest was written, the extermination of Indigenous peoples continued, and a dehumanized Black workforce was shackled to the task of building a new empire.

Few people realize that Indian constables, who policed increasingly displaced Native populations during the early stages of US colonialism, and slave patrols, which captured Black slaves who had escaped their white masters, were this country's first police. To understand these historical origins—along with the present state of law enforcement and the mechanics of the prison-industrial complex—is to understand that the role of the police in the United States has not changed substantially over time, though it has been rebranded. The main function of US policing remains the same: the management of people who have historically been identified as human resources, or human hindrances, by the prevailing power structure.

Law enforcement, in functionality, remains the same as it ever was.

Despite profound moments of cooperation and shared struggle between Black and Indigenous movements—which have included such moments as Indigenous people harboring and building community with escaped and former slaves—there is much to reconcile about the intersections of our shared histories. Some believe, for example, that Ray Robinson, a Black civil rights activist, was killed by members of AIM in 1973, during the siege at Wounded Knee. Robinson, who reportedly joined the protesters, disappeared during the chaos of those events. While AIM members claim that Robinson left of his own volition, some have held fast to the belief that AIM members, suspecting that Robinson was a government spy, killed him as a matter of tactical security. Regardless of which narrative is true, there is certainly a historical grounding for suspicion and disconnect between Black and Indigenous people.

In my own experience, I have found that dialogues about Native and Black relations often lack a shared historical understanding. This is unsurprising, given that both Black and Native people are constantly at odds with the erasure of their respective histories in the United States. The work of telling our own stories and forcing honest dialogues about the harms perpetrated against our peoples is at times exhausting. The history of our experiences is softened, sanitized and whitewashed in classrooms and popular entertainment. But living on the front lines of our own struggles sometimes means missing the opportunity to share in the pursuit of social and political transformation.

Even in social justice circles, I have encountered few Black people who are familiar with the role that the so-called Buffalo Soldiers played in Native displacement during westward expansion. However, in Native communities, stories of the Black soldiers who fought for the North during the Civil War and were sent West in the war's aftermath have not been forgotten. The role of Black soldiers in the subjugation of Native peoples was viewed by some as a point of pride. "We made the West," Tenth Cavalry Pvt. Henry McCombs, a Black Buffalo soldier, declared in 1895. "[We] defeated the hostile tribes of Indians; and made the country safe to live in."[4] And while stories of the bravery exhibited by Black soldiers during the Civil War are well-known, stories of Black soldiers participating in campaigns of violence against Native people, including the government's 1890–91 Wounded Knee campaign, are far less discussed outside of Native communities.

Similarly, one will rarely hear discussion, in Native circles, of the sad reality that some Native people owned Black slaves until the practice was ended by treaty at the close of the Civil War. While the institution was rare among Native people—with less than 3 percent of Natives owning slaves at the height of the practice[5]—it is nonetheless a dark stain in Native history, and one that most are not eager to revisit. With Black people in the United States attempting to build forward in the aftermath of slavery, living with the cultural memory of its horrors, a failure to fully speak to this entanglement of Native culture with one of this country's darkest realities has no doubt created a barrier to dialogue and contributed to various rifts between Native and Black populations.

While many Native people question the collective blame heaped upon over 500 nations for the actions of the small fraction of the Native population that owned slaves, it is important to remember that Blackness is likewise not a monolith. Native people, like Black people, are often understood collectively. This is a reality that is also experienced by Black Americans, despite their varied origins, and any dismantling of these socially constructed ideas can only occur through dialogue.

While Native and Black people have at times fought alongside each other,[6] recognition of the ways in which both groups have replicated the harms of colonialism is clearly necessary if the two groups are to build forward in solidarity.

As William C. Anderson, a Black journalist (and the author of Chapter 6 of this book) who frequently addresses issues of race, told me: "It's important we work together to seek collective liberation. However, we have to do that in a way that engages both anti-Blackness and Native genocide. We have to work together in sustainable ways that are real. ... We have to build with one another, not against. We should do so in a way that recognizes grievances but still puts freedom first."

A process of social transformation, which not only acknowledges the harms experienced on both sides, but also seeks to root out the reasons why we have at times failed one another, would no doubt be a massive undertaking. However, recognizing that harmed individuals and communities in turn commit harms, often in the same rhythms, many believe that a process of healing is long overdue. In some places, it may have already begun.

The Language of Oppression

With some Black and Brown activists working to build coalitions, conflicts still manifest themselves. At times these conflicts are grounded not only in a failure to reconcile history but in a failure to establish an actual language of understanding. Questions about the vocabulary of both our suffering and liberation emerge and stir discord between potential allies.

Is it acceptable for Native people to use a #NativeLivesMatter variation of the #BlackLivesMatter hashtag? Does the language of "colonization" apply to both the Black and Indigenous experiences? Is language addressing the particular struggles of Native people adequately incorporated into conversations about police violence?

Page May is a young Black organizer with We Charge Genocide in Chicago, a co-founder of the Assata's Daughters collective, and co-author of Chapter 11 of this book. May has been confronted with the complexities of Black and Native vocabularies of oppression in movement spaces. She noted to Truthout that "in Chicago, and elsewhere, there's a lot of conversation in Black communities about naming our own struggles." While these conversations do afford a level of separateness, May does not believe that making historical and cultural distinctions is necessarily harmful to solidarity efforts. "I hope [these conversations] aren't read as Black people trying to distance themselves from Indigenous struggle," she explains. In actuality, May says, she worries "about Black people appropriating Indigenous struggle with words like 'decolonization' and 'genocide.' Indigenous people deserve their own grammar of suffering, as do Black people."

In contrast to Indigenous people, who have always existed in resistance to erasure under colonization, Page says, "Blackness is always positioned as alienated from a place of origin—as having no Nativeness, as though Blacks are produced through dungeons—in a state of natal alienation." In May's view, this narrative othering, which forces Blackness out of any context of its own, holds Black people in a chattel state, shuffled from exploitation to exploitation without any cultural narrative but the experience of social death.

While May speaks of a cyclical narrative that entraps Blackness, some who come from Native backgrounds feel that their struggle is wholly erased in the popular dialogue. "When I tell people the numbers and explain that police kill us at a higher rate than they kill anyone," a young Native woman told me, "they act like that can't be real. Like the statistics must be skewed in some way. I just want to yell at them: Yes, they are skewed! White supremacy skewed them by killing so many of us that you don't notice us die anymore!"

But the lack of notice, this young woman explained, is not the most disturbing thought she attaches to these exchanges. "The worst thought, what I try not to believe, is that people, both other people of color and white people, that they do understand, and don't care, because people have accepted the idea of us fading out. Like it's already happened, so we're not worth fighting for."

The young Native woman I spoke to, who asked that her name not be shared publicly, is not alone in her concern that Native struggles with police violence are not being widely recognized or discussed. As Derek Royden has written: "The Black Lives Matter movement has made a significant impact in part because African Americans are a visible presence in America's large urban areas. By contrast, Native Americans are more easily ignored since they often live in more rural areas and on reservations."[7]

Aware of such concerns, Page May speaks to the issue of Native erasure by insisting that "we have to take time to highlight the Indigenous resistance that is a part of our struggle. There is a long history of Black and Indigenous people working together to support one another's movements."

While May feels that there is great importance in forming distinct cultural frames around our differing experiences, she notes that "the goal of giving unique names to our struggles is not exceptionalism. It's being better prepared for understanding what actual solidarity means."

Sharing Struggle in Chicago

While there have been numerous intersections in the work of Black and Indigenous activists in the last year, my clearest view of what's possible has come through such efforts in my own city.

When the Black Lives Matter movement brought young people around the country into the streets, Chicago's youth were already there, waiting to seize the moment. Young Black people working with groups like BYP 100, We Charge Genocide, and Circles and Ciphers were already pursuing community-based solutions to violence, and pushing back against the violence of the police state. But even with young people organizing well beyond their years, the tasks and opportunities suddenly at hand were massive. I had no expectations of being invited to play a role in a Black-led movement against anti-Black police violence, but the relationships I had already built with young Black people in our collective efforts to organize against police violence quickly landed me in an ongoing supportive role.

As a direct action trainer, I led workshops and sat in on planning sessions to help young people prepare for their marches, sit-ins and artistic protests. By showing up and making a concerted effort not to impose myself, I was able to build trust with young leaders, who in time relied on me to help build staging grounds for their actions. As our relationships deepened, I felt a profound connection with some of the young leaders who were lifting their voices in our streets. Their skills quickly expanded, and before long, instead of trying to impart knowledge, I was collaborating with them on how we could broaden community networks of tactical knowledge.

One of those efforts took the form of the Rad Ed Project.[8] As someone who has done a fair amount of traveling as both a direct action trainer and a workshop participant, I know that some of the most exciting opportunities for sharing and learning protest tactics happen in action camps. These camps—where activists sharpen skills ranging from facilitation to blockades work—are often weeklong excursions that require airfare and the ability to take time away from school, work and family responsibilities for days at a time. The result of such constraints is that, quite predictably, these environments are predominantly white.

So some of us set out to create a local solution in Chicago. Through Rad Ed, we sought to create a number of weekend-long sessions, as well as a series of shorter skill-sharing sessions, that would allow participants—particularly youth of color—to pick up some of the skills that they might acquire at an action camp. Some great skill shares were organized to meet those goals, but something else happened as well—something that wasn't a named objective of the project.

We created a space where Black and Indigenous people could reflect on our shared struggle, and effectively built together in common cause.

The original idea behind the project was to bring in highly experienced trainers to prepare young people to be skill sharers in their communities. Toward that end, we invited Remy, a Diné, Navajo, arts trainer from a highly respected direct-action training organization called the Ruckus Society, to help run our first weekend-long event. Prior to the training, I made clear to Remy that he would be walking into a challenging room, sharing space with junior high school students, teenagers and 20-somethings who would push back if their politics and lived experiences weren't respected. While the project was fueled by the momentum of Black Lives Matter, we had opened the project to all young people of color who might want to attend, and the applications we received reflected a much greater diversity than we would have expected. Black, Brown, Indigenous and mixed, our participants were community members who wanted to show up to learn how to bring movement skills back to their communities during a time of upheaval, and it was their intentions that we needed to honor.

We only expected to have Remy with us for a single weekend, but the experiences we shared that weekend led him to return to the city within a few short months, to help organize the project's second major workshop.

At the end of the first weekend-long training, which focused on artful protest, we carried out an action in support of the reparations ordinance for survivors of police torture in Chicago. The banners our attendees created for that action were the subject of a great deal of discussion during the course of the weekend, as we talked through Native struggle, anti-Blackness and how oppressed people could build forward together. We all learned from each other in that space, both from the lived experiences and insights of young people, and from the wisdom that Remy imparted from his experiences combating genocide on multiple fronts.

He would frequently remind us of the intersections between stolen land, stolen lives and stolen liberty. "The intersections of both our struggles are well-documented outside of mainstream education," he told me, reminding me that we could not allow the stories of our peoples to be separated into disconnected narratives. "There's a history and a spirit of our cooperative resistance that this country's history books try to rob us of," he said. It was our need for each other, he reasoned, that led the power structure to paint us into our own corners.

By the end of the weekend, we created two banners for the reparations action. One bore the refrain of the movement for reparations—"Reparations Now!"—and one bore our own demand, "Transformation Now!"

It was not enough, our participants reasoned, to seek to make the injured whole, because real change would require a new unity and a total reorientation of society.

At the close of the action that we carried out that Monday, outside of City Hall, Page May, who co-organized the event, called those in attendance together in a large circle. She welcomed torture victims and Black youth into the center to join hands. She also invited members of a community whose abuse at the hands of police had recently been highlighted in the media. Then came something unexpected. Without any advance discussion, May widened the theme of the moment by welcoming all Indigenous people in attendance to join those standing in the center of the circle. She emphasized the struggles of Black people in Chicago, where Black youth are attacked, harassed and killed by police at a higher rate than any other demographic, but also paid respect to the fact that we were all standing on stolen land, and that Native people have continuously been victimized by the state on a massive scale, nationwide.

In that moment, the connectivity of our struggles as victims of state violence was manifested in direct action. From Columbus' torture and enslavement of the Taino people, which launched the horrors of the transatlantic slave trade, to the plantations and death marches our peoples were condemned to, and the internalized and replicated oppressions that have at times torn us apart, I could feel who we all were, and who we were to each other. If only for a moment, the violence of white supremacy was met with a unified chorus of resistance, as those of us in the center locked hands, forming an inner circle that faced the larger crowd. We led the larger circle in a chant, calling out Black freedom fighter Assata Shakur's words: "We have a duty to fight for our freedom! We have a duty to win! We must love each other and protect each other! We have nothing to lose but our chains!"

After bringing her students to the action that night in lieu of classroom time, renowned Black activist and educator Mariame Kaba, one of my dearest mentors, wrote on Facebook: "In the freezing cold, there was such powerful and healing energy all around me. I could feel the energy in my bones. I felt truly lucky to be there. I am so glad that I got to bring my students along. Each of them expressed a similar feeling. These are the intangible moments that are part of organizing. They are organic. Tonight was a special night. When we win the reparations ordinance, I will look back at this gathering as a seminal moment."

Within a few months, we won the fight: Chicago became the first city in the country to attain reparations for victims of police torture. And while the fight was long and hard, I will always remember the campaign from the center of that circle, where we transcended the divide-and-conquer mentality of a power structure that wants us to view ourselves as more different than alike, and the would-be pundits who benefit from reinforcing such divisions.

We stood together, and we believed that we could win—and we were right.

Yes, it was just one moment at one action, and as builders of culture and community we obviously have a lot of truth and history to reconcile, a lot of bickering to overcome and a lot of bridges to build. But many times, experiencing and falling in love with what's possible is what begins the journey of transformation. While I agree with William C. Anderson's assessment that "If we're going to help one another, we have to be honest about the history and the future," I also agree with my friend Page May, who once told me, "We have to inhabit our history, but we also have to inhabit our dreams."

I dream of freedom—for us all. And I believe we can get there together.

14.

A New Year's Resolution: Don't Call the Police[1]

Mike Ludwig

Looking for a New Year's resolution? If you haven't found one already, there's never been a better time to resolve not to call the cops.

This resolution is more than a boycott or a political protest. It's the beginning of a thought process and a dialogue, both internal and external, that challenges us to build new relationships with our friends, family and neighbors. It's a spark in the imagination that leads us to dream about a free world.

For those of us who weren't already aware, the events of 2014 made it clear that the police do more harm than good, especially in communities of color. From the streets of Ferguson to Berkeley and New York City, people from all walks of life have been loudly resisting the power of police, who all too often prove themselves to be racist, armed and dangerous. At our rallies, we chant the names of the dead: Mike Brown, Tamir Rice, Eric Garner and countless others.

Some cops just bully people, but others kill, and the justice system lets them get away with it. In 2012, a study by the Malcolm X Grassroots Movement found that police summarily executed more than 313 black people that year—an average of one every 28 hours.[2]

This is not a new problem. Police routinely target certain people—

particularly people of color (especially men) and gender-nonconforming people—for minor crimes such as drug possession or loitering, or for no crime at all, simply stopping them for "driving while Black" or "walking while woman."[3]

Last year, the American Civil Liberties Union found that Blacks were 3.7 times more likely to be arrested for marijuana possession than whites, despite similar rates of drug use.[4] In some counties, that number reaches 30 times higher.[5]

As a result, people of color and other marginalized people are disproportionately warehoused in our vast prison system, which tears families apart and only exacerbates cycles of poverty, crime and violence.

Police officers are all individuals, and it's impossible to say that they are all bad at their jobs. However, police have all sworn to uphold laws that systematically disenfranchise marginalized and working people for the benefit of the rich and powerful.

Consider Ferguson, where one young man participating in the protests in August told me that local police often harass and even ticket young Black men for failing to walk on a sidewalk on a street that doesn't even have sidewalks.[6] If they can't pay that ticket, the court fees add up, and they could end up in jail, separated from their families and livelihoods.

A few days later, the media began citing a report by local public defenders that detailed how racial profiling, along with a local legal system designed to keep people wrapped up in its web, fills the coffers of the local municipalities in the St. Louis area that pay the wages of the cops who are supposed to protect and serve everyone equally.[7]

This may not be news to you. Perhaps you have already resolved not to call the cops because you are unfairly criminalized by the color of your skin, your personal behavior or your gender presentation. You may know from experience that the police are better at escalating than de-escalating situations that range from domestic conflicts to political protests or even the sale of a few loose cigarettes.

If you have not yet made this resolution, consider that not calling the police raises some difficult but important questions. It forces us to consider whom we feel potentially threatened by and why, and how we are defining "safety." Do we feel unsafe in working-class neighbor-hoods, or around people with certain styles of dress or colors of skin? What prejudices ground this fear?

Resolving not to call the police inspires us to consider the alter-natives. Instead of calling the police to complain about a loud party at your neighbor's house, you could address your neighbors directly, with the intent of having a constructive conversation about each oth-er's needs. Talking with our neighbors about taking responsibility for keeping our communities safe and happy helps us learn from each other and establish trust: the first steps toward building relationships that are strong enough to confront more complicated problems, such as bullying or domestic violence.

Violence is the most serious challenge. If you feel that your safety is threatened, and the best option to avoid being harmed is calling the police, you should do it. Resolving not to call the police is not a rule, just a way to think outside the box. Rules are for the cops, not for us.

There are, however, proven models for dealing with even difficult social issues without involving the police. One example: Police in cit-ies arrest more people for drug offenses than for most other crimes,[8] and a vast majority of all drug arrests are for possession, not sale or manufacturing.[9] The harm reduction movement[10] has effectively im-plemented many community-based strategies to reduce the harms caused by drug use while empowering drug users and non–drug users alike to work together toward healing and treating addiction.[11]

Throwing people in jail for using drugs causes harm by seriously interrupting their lives, while at the same time reinforcing the stigma around drug use that drives people in need of help into the shadows. Harm reduction does the exact opposite.

Across the country and around the world, people are using mod-els of "transformative" and "restorative" justice to address offenses such as violence, sexual assault and domestic abuse without involving the police.[12] These models use cooperative processes, with survivors of the offense often directly involved, to repair the harm and trauma caused by the offense, while holding offenders accountable to survi-vors and working with them to transform their behavior.

Taking responsibility for keeping our communities safe and seeking justice on our own terms is not an easy task. It may sound radically ideal, like a dream. This dream, however, is already shared by a critical mass of people. It's a dream of a world without police and prisons, a world where the struggle for true freedom is explicitly connected to our own collective empowerment and mutual compassion.

Keep this world in your heart. Dream beyond the police.

15.

Community Groups Work to Provide Emergency Medical Alternatives, Separate From Police[1]

Candice Bernd

When Jens Rushing was working as an EMT for a 911 service in one small Texas city, he was dispatched on a call where he witnessed a man experiencing a mental health crisis. He remembers how the police officer who accompanied him wanted to cuff the man's hands behind his back and force him, face down, to the ground, until he "calmed down."

"[The officer was] completely unaware of the threat of positional asphyxia, of which people die," Rushing told Truthout. "We had to argue with him to get the patient away from [the police] and let us [EMTs] do it our way, chemically sedating the patient rather than physically restraining the patient, and actually tending to them as a patient, rather than as a person committing the 'crime' of having an acute psychotic episode."

Rushing says that during his time as an EMT for this small city, police officers were dispatched with him on almost every call, sometimes becoming unnecessarily confrontational and problematic—especially, he said, on calls in which patients were struggling with mental illnesses. In February 2012, he left that city to work for 911 services in Arlington, Texas, for a few months. Now, he works as an ambulance paramedic for a Texas hospital he prefers not to name.

Though Rushing says there are occasions when having cops arrive first to secure the scene and guarantee paramedics' safety can be useful, he says police can and do make unstable situations worse. He told Truthout he's witnessed several officers physically and verbally abuse people.

"Occasionally [police] do make matters worse. I don't see a way of changing that working relationship outside of changing the fundamental structure of the role that police play in our society," Rushing said.

Issues like the ones Rushing observed are leading some communities to find alternative solutions to traditional 911 first responders and emergency medical services (EMS), as a means of minimizing contact with the police in tense and volatile situations. Organizers and activists across the country are working to build first-response models that rely on community members taking medical knowledge into their own hands—and often acting to prevent medical crises before they happen.

Oakland Organizers Build Community Power With Medical Cohort Training

In September 2015, organizers with the Oakland chapter of Critical Resistance (CR), which works to abolish prisons and policing, launched the Oakland Power Projects (OPP).[2] The OPP initiative aims to build "the capacity for Oakland residents to reject police and policing as the default response to harm and to highlight or create alternatives that actually work by identifying current harms, amplifying existing resources, and developing new practices that do not rely on policing solutions," according to CR's website.

At the time of writing, the first Power Project is taking shape in the form of an "Anti-Policing Community Health Workers Cohort." The cohort are scheduled to participate in a training series that will be conducted during five Saturday sessions. In these workshops, community street medics and health care workers of all backgrounds will work to build residents' skills and knowledge so they can provide health care for one another without relying on police.

"What we need are resources to build community strength from the ground up," said CR development director Jess Heaney, who helps coordinate the OPPs. She said the City of Oakland was unwilling to help maintain community building by investing in neighborhoods. "They also won't invest in a quality of resources. So we can do it on our own, at the grassroots level."

The OPP initiative hopes to build upon the victories of the abolition and anti-police organizing efforts of the Stop the Injunctions Coalition (STIC), which successfully pressured the Oakland Police Department, City Attorney and City Council for more than six years to stop enforcing or expanding gang injunctions in Oakland. STIC scored a decisive victory in March 2015, when the Alameda County Superior Court dismissed two civil gang injunctions that would have allowed the targeted policing of people or communities suspected of gang activity.[3]

Now, organizers are hoping to build on this momentum to grow their own resources for addressing harm, as a means of divesting from policing. CR organizers in Oakland conducted a survey in 2014, soliciting responses from Oakland residents and allies of STIC about their experiences with the police, and asking them about how they think Oakland can best build alternatives to policing structures. These community members overwhelmingly said they wanted access to health care resources that weren't connected to policing, as well as alternative first-response models for emergency health crises.[4]

"People wanted to have first responders come when they needed 911, but the cops showing up there and cordoning off the scene, and actually stopping people from getting health care until cops were able to do what they wanted to do, was negatively impacting the community's experience in passing moments of crisis," Heaney said.

Heaney says that once CR understood what the community wanted, she and other organizers reached out to street medics and health care workers of varying stripes, from emergency room doctors and nurses to local herbal healers. From their dialogue the idea of a medical cohort training was established.

"This idea of 'knowing your options' emerged, so we started working on a health workers' training that would provide 'know your options' education to Oakland community organizations," Heaney said. "So that when a moment came and people needed health care, whether it's a long-term health care plan ... or in times of crisis, people would feel confident, would have the skills and the understanding and resources available, and the relationships necessary, to not have to go to a place where cops would be present or cops would be first responders."

CR has already been working in coalition with other national organizations, including the Ella Baker Center, to provide workshops focused on reducing harm and conflict, and reimagining community safety, without relying on the police. With their first Oakland Power Project, they hope to combine their previous workshops about abolishing the prison-industrial complex with medical information and training, including not only preventive care for common issues like high blood pressure, diabetes and minor injuries, but also emergency skills like CPR and treating gunshot or stabbing wounds. Trainers also hope to distribute medical kits that community members can use for first response to emergencies, to help prevent calls to 911.

Aside from emergency care, the training's other key focuses will be mental health and de-escalation tactics, as well as chronic health conditions, with trainees participating in building distinct medical kits and lists of resources for their preferred focus area. The hope is that trainees will then become trainers in their focus area and continue to distribute their newfound knowledge within their own networks, workplaces and neighborhoods throughout Oakland.

Rushing, the ambulance paramedic based in Texas, is sympathetic to the need for initiatives like the OPPs. (He formerly volunteered as a street medic for Occupy Dallas in the fall of 2011, when the group was camping and actively organizing in the city.)

"There are many people divided amongst race and class lines who can and can't call 911 freely, without fear, with or without the assumption that the people coming are public servants who are going to help you, or people that you try to avoid at all costs," he said, referring to the fact that people of color are often targeted by police in violent and lethal ways, resulting in a hesitancy among these communities to call the police or 911—even when they urgently need assistance.

He added that the need for the program also betrays a stark injustice in the way public resources are utilized. "Everybody should absolutely have access to emergency health care and the level of care that paramedics are able to offer, with our training and the advanced medical equipment and techniques that we have on our ambulances," Rushing said.

However, emergency medical services have always occupied an odd place in the health care landscape. Rushing noted that most of his fellow EMS workers are sympathetic to police because they tend to identify more with emergency service providers like firefighters and cops, or even the military, than with other health care workers.

"[EMTs] can be on the fire truck or on the ambulance on a day-by-day basis. It depends on the city and the department," Rushing said. "And a fire department has always been a 'paramilitary organization,' in that it was originally made up of veterans, especially after the Civil War and world wars, and retained much of the power structure from the military."

However, some groups are finding a "third way" between working within the system, as Rushing has, and working completely outside of it, as CR organizers are building toward doing. This approach—working with the system in a partial way—aims to minimize police contact and provide alternative forms of EMS care.

Eugene's "CAHOOTS" Shares Dispatch With Police While Minimizing Contact

In Eugene, Oregon, White Bird Clinic's Crisis Assistance Helping Out On The Streets (CAHOOTS) program[5] is a mobile crisis-intervention service that shares a central dispatch with the Eugene Police Department (EPD) and is fully integrated into, and funded by, the City of Eugene's public safety services.

The service is dispatched through the city's non-emergency police, fire and ambulance call center, but is designed to provide an alternative to law enforcement action whenever possible for cases of non-criminal drug and substance abuse, poverty-related issues and mental health crises. A majority of CAHOOTS clients, about 60 percent, are homeless.

The service was first created in 1989 as a collaboration between White Bird Clinic, a nonprofit social service organization, and the City of Eugene, to address the needs of the city's homeless population and people living with addiction or chronic mental illness, among other marginalized groups.

The CAHOOTS van dispatches between 11 a.m. and 3 a.m., seven days a week, with at least one nurse or EMT and one crisis worker who provide free first-response services to people experiencing a broad array of non-criminal crises. The CAHOOTS team can provide non-emergency medical care and basic first aid, as well as mental crisis intervention services, including case assessment, referral and advocacy. CAHOOTS-trained teams also routinely provide counseling services, mediation in disputes and transportation to social services.

"A lot of citizens that I think would otherwise not be calling and getting support ... because they'd be afraid of the type of responses they might get, I think feel more comfortable calling us because they know that we're a human-service response," said Benjamin Brubaker, a White Bird Clinic administrative staff member and CAHOOTS team crisis worker. "In most municipalities, you have police, fire, ambulance, and that's what you're going to get if you call 911 or a non-emergency number, and here in Eugene, we've been able to work with the local police department to build this kind of fourth human-service option."

Brubaker said that the acronym CAHOOTS is the team's tongue-in-cheek way of being up-front with the community about the fact that they partner with the EPD in certain situations. "We're going to show up on the scene, maybe where the police are there," Brubaker said. "But how that's been broken down for the folks out on the streets, and how they kind of see that is: The police are there. They don't really want the police to be there. They call us and we show up and say, 'OK guys, we got this,' and the police clear out."

Brubaker told Truthout that typically people call up the non-emergency police number, and the EPD determines whether or not the call is appropriate for a CAHOOTS team to handle. If it is, the EPD will dispatch the CAHOOTS van directly to a scene. But if the EPD determines there's a criminal and/or dangerous element involved in a situation, many times they'll respond first and have a CAHOOTS team staged nearby, or call a team later to take over for them.

"We're not there to do what we call 'inflicting help.' We want to assist people in finding their own answers, because we believe ultimately that everybody already has the answers inside of themselves for the situations that they're in," Brubaker said. "We're going to sometimes have to call someone [the EPD] who can 'inflict help,' but we try to make sure that that doesn't happen very often."

As the CAHOOTS program has developed its relationship with the City of Eugene over the years, the service has grown so much that it now responds to more than 9,000 calls every year. In October 2014, the program announced its expansion into the neighboring city of Springfield. Rushing thinks the CAHOOTS model is helping to fill the gaps in health care services that traditional emergency response "can't or doesn't cover." He told Truthout that, in his experience, about 90 percent of the calls he's been on have been non-emergencies.

"There's a lot of people who have a lot of chronic illnesses that don't need a trip to the [emergency room], but still need medical attention," he said. "So [a similar model] could potentially be able to relieve the strain on an EMS system, which would be great, and also provide better access to health care for a lot of more vulnerable people."

But Rushing cautioned that nonprofit models that are embedded with the police might be more feasible in places like Eugene, which is predominantly white, than in other areas with higher demographics of people of color.

"I'm sure the demographic of Eugene would have something to do with how successful the program is. Certainly in a place ... with majority-minority populations and a police department with, let's charitably say, a non-progressive record, it would definitely be more difficult to integrate a service like that with the police department and with the community at large," Rushing said.

According to the CAHOOTS team's own internal analysis of the calls they handle and other internal data collected from January 1 through June 8, the CAHOOTS team expects to take approximately 6,000 additional calls on average by the end of 2015.

The team estimates that, so far in 2015, about 11.4 percent of the calls they've taken have involved providing direct assistance to EPD officers in the field, and 3.6 percent of their calls have involved CAHOOTS workers directly assisting EMS workers. CAHOOTS crisis workers provide counseling services in about 64 percent of calls in which they are not providing transportation to social services or the hospital. The program provides medical services in 22 percent of these non-transport calls. The remaining 14 percent of those calls involve substance abuse issues.

Additionally, the CAHOOTS team analyzed dispatch data from their own cases as well as EPD data and estimated that, in 2012 and 2013, the CAHOOTS service handled more than half of all cases involving personal welfare safety checks and transport to social services.

CAHOOTS is a win in terms of the municipal budget, too. Citing the city's own estimates, CAHOOTS workers estimate that their service saves the EPD over $4.5 million annually. The organization has also calculated that their work adds up to more than $1 million in ER and EMS diversion savings (without including the cost of ambulance services).

"There's a large lack of foresight as far as spending goes in governments across the country. They have a hard time spending money on mental health and substance abuse issues to help actually treat [patients]," Brubaker said. "Instead, what's happening is a lot of that money is just getting transferred to law enforcement [and] legal systems in order to deal with those individuals, where really what I think needs to happen is more money needs to be in mental health and substance abuse treatment."

Brubaker hopes other municipalities will consider replicating the Eugene/CAHOOTS model of partnering city services with social service nonprofits to provide care in non-emergency situations—instead of relying on city police departments to do so. He noted that when there is an assumption that police will always be involved in emergency services, many people simply do not seek help.

"I have countless examples of when I was able to be of service to folks who really needed it that may not have reached out for services if they thought anyone else but CAHOOTS was going to show up," Brubaker said.

16.

Building Community Safety: Practical Steps Toward Liberatory Transformation[1]

Ejeris Dixon

"Mom, when you were growing up, did you ever call the police?"

"I can't remember any time that we did."

"What did you do if something violent happened?"

"It depended on the situation. Often we could send for the uncles, brothers, fathers or other family members of people involved to interrupt violence. However, there was this time when we had this family that lived on our block, where the husband was attacking his wife. And people were fed up, so some men in the community with standing—a minister, teacher, doctor, etc.—decided to intervene. Those men stopped by the house to let the husband know that they wouldn't tolerate his behavior and it needed to stop."

My mom grew up in New Orleans in the 1940s, 1950s and 1960s. Her entire life was marked by experiences of state violence and Jim Crow segregation. The police, white citizens' councils and the Klan intermingled and formed the backbone of a racist political and economic system. Her experiences were not unique. Historically and currently, most marginalized communities—including Black people, poor people, queer and trans people, and people with disabilities—have experienced violence and discrimination from police, emergency services and the legal system.

Just as the use of state violence against Black communities is not new, neither are the ideas of transformative justice or community accountability. Transformative justice and community accountability are terms that describe ways to address violence without relying upon police or prisons. These approaches often work to prevent violence, to intervene when harm is occurring, to hold people accountable, and to transform individuals and society to build safer communities. These strategies are some of the only options that marginalized communities have for addressing harm.

The work of transformative justice can happen in a variety of ways. Some groups support survivors by helping them to identify their needs and boundaries, while simultaneously ensuring that their attackers agree to these boundaries and atone for the harm they caused. Other groups create safe spaces and sanctuaries to support people who are escaping from violence. There are also community campaigns designed to educate community members on the specific dynamics of violence, how to prevent it, and what community-based programs are available.

As the powerfully inspiring movement to end anti-Black state violence continues to grow, we must ensure that our work toward community safety receives the same amount of attention and diligence. As a person who has survived multiple forms of violence, I know that ending state violence alone will not keep me, my family, my friends or my community safe. I'm excited by the campaigns that organizers are pursuing to divert money away from police departments and into community services. However, I want us to push this work one step further. I believe we can build community safety systems that will one day operate independently from the police and all government systems.

The process of building community safety poses some critical questions to our movements.

What is the world that we want?

How will we begin to define safety?

How do we build the skills to address harm and violence?

How do we create the trust needed for communities to rely on each other for mutual support?

I'd like to offer some answers to these questions in the form of principles for building community safety strategies. By acting on these principles, everyone can take steps to decrease our reliance on police and prisons.

Relationship Building

From 2005 to 2010, I had the privilege of serving as the founding program coordinator of the Safe OUTside the System Collective at the Audre Lorde Project. During that time I worked alongside other queer and trans people of color living in Central Brooklyn to create a campaign that would address state violence and anti-LGBTQ violence without relying on the criminal legal system. During that time I learned that the process of building community-based strategies can fundamentally reshape our ways of engaging with each other.

Violence and oppression break community ties and breed fear and distrust. At its core, the work of creating safety means building meaningful, accountable relationships within our neighborhoods and communities. Within the S.O.S. Collective, we made it a point to do outreach in the immediate area after incidents of violence. While it often felt terrifying to talk about the work of preventing and ending violence against LGBTQ people of color, we built strong allies and had life-changing conversations.

Time and time again I've known people who were saved by the relationships they built. I've seen people who were selling drugs for survival intervene in anti-trans violence because they had relationships with their neighbors. I know friends who've helped their neighbors escape from violent relationships based on the connections they have built together.

If and when violence occurs, it's the people who live within the closest proximity who are most likely able to help us, and vice versa. Relationship building doesn't have to involve old-school door knocking. It can be as simple as attending community events, saying hello and introducing yourself to your neighbors, or inviting your neighbors to events that you organize. It can be the act of talking to your noisy neighbor as opposed to calling the cops. It's about the necessity of meeting the businesses and storeowners in your immediate area and on routes that you frequently use.

This strategy is not without complications.

For many people, particularly women and gender-nonconforming people, the act of engaging with strangers can open us up to harassment and even violence. At the same time, these challenges shouldn't prevent us from building relationships; they may merely shift the ways in which we go about it. Attending community events is also a great way to build relationships.

We must also be cognizant of the way that class, educational privilege and gentrification can impact relationship building. Gentrification is its own form of violence within many low-income neighborhoods. Many gentrifiers/newcomers act fearful and do not shop within their communities, attend events, or build relationships with their neighbors. Gentrifiers/newcomers who are also movement leaders tend to create movements and strategies that are not grounded within the lived experiences of the people most impacted by violence.

While I don't believe that we can separate ourselves from our privileges, I think we can leverage them toward justice. My educational privilege and relationships mean that I know a lot of lawyers and have knowledge about our rights during police encounters. I've made sure to share "know your rights" information with my neighbors, observe the cops alongside my neighbors, and give legal referrals. Through these moments I've been able to build stronger relationships with my neighbors and deepen trust.

Bold, Small Experiments

Some of the most innovative transformative justice and community accountability projects have come from bold, small experiments. The Safe OUTside the System Collective started from the audacity of a small team of people who believed that we could prevent and intervene in violent situations without the police. During our weekly meetings, for over a year, we discussed our experiences of violence and brainstormed responses. At that time, LGBTQ people of color were reporting physical attacks to us at least once a month, and there were two to three murders per year in Central Brooklyn.

Meanwhile, the NYPD was operating like an occupying army. It was common to walk home from the subway and see officers stationed on every block, or large groups of police officers walking down the street. We had no choice but to create a community safety campaign. Our campaign recruited and trained local businesses and organizations in how to recognize, prevent and intervene in violence without relying on law enforcement.

At first we had no idea how to work on this, but we researched and experimented. We talked with the business owners themselves to understand how they already addressed violence and worked with them to ensure that their strategies included LGBTQ people of color. At the time, we did not think we were doing something innovative. We just knew we needed to build new structures for our ultimate survival.

I believe that bold, small experiments rise and fall based on two fairly simple ideas: planning and perseverance. We have to be accountable enough to continue our experiments, measure them, hold ourselves to high standards, and believe in them. Even within completely volunteer projects, we are using a very valuable resource: time. And it is often those of us with the least money, time and privilege who end up disproportionately putting our time into movement work. So as we continue our experiments, we need to talk about what our goals are, where we're trying to get, what resources are needed, and how we're going to distribute those resources equitably.

The question, therefore, is: What can you help build? What conversations can you start to increase the safety of your community? What new structures or collaborations will you create to decrease your reliance on the criminal legal system? Perhaps you want to think about one form of violence to work on and build your knowledge from there. You could start simply by having a dinner with your friends, family and chosen family to discuss how you all can better support each other. Or you could raise the issue of police violence and harassment at your next tenants' association meeting and see if there's a way that your neighbors want to engage with each other as opposed to the police. Next, you could research ways that people can get emergency medical assistance outside of 911. The possibilities are endless.

No matter how small they are, our experiments should aspire to center the experiences of the most marginalized folks within our communities. One of the major challenges of the movements of the 1960s and 1970s was their inability to fully hold and implement an intersectional analysis. We need to work to make sure that our bold experiments are centering the experiences of Black people, people with disabilities, trans people, poor people, undocumented people, and all marginalized people. Starting small gives us the opportunity to collectively imagine community safety responses without telling anyone to wait their turn.

Taking Time to Build Skills

In order to truly ensure safety for our communities, we also need to ensure that we have the necessary skills. One of our largest failures in this arena seems to stem from arrogance. There are times when we believe we inherently have the skills to address harm, simply because we have a strong political analysis or a strong desire to address harm. There's a substantial distinction between having skills and learning skills, between being experts and practicing.

In activist and progressive communities, we're accustomed to attending one training or reading one essay and then declaring ourselves leaders and educators on an issue. I believe that the notion of instant expertise is contrary to our liberatory values. Safety is not a product that we can package and market. Community safety is not a certification that we place on our resumes. We have the invitation to practice with one of our most precious resources, our lives. In a world that is already trying to kill us with a multitude of oppressive strategies, we must be deliberate and vigilant to honor where we each are in our journeys.

I've spent the last 10 years practicing verbal de-escalation strategies to address violence on the street, at events, and at actions and protests. I am constantly learning and growing. Every incident is different; sometimes I can reduce or defuse conflict, and other times I fail miserably. The strategies or tactics that work in one instance can go horribly wrong in others, even under similar conditions. Intervening in violence in the moment is inherently about using nonverbal communication to read, communicate, or negotiate safety. With each incident I tell myself that I am developing my instincts and that by practicing I learn, despite the outcome.

We must practice community safety much as one practices an instrument or a sport: in slow, measurable and deliberate ways. Only by practicing can we build the knowledge we need to defuse and address conflict within our communities.

We can also learn a great deal if we are open to engaging with people who have different politics than we do. I left the S.O.S. Collective in 2010 because it was time for new leadership, and I was ready to continue learning in other settings. I took a job at a large LGBTQ anti-violence organization that wasn't involved with transformative justice or community accountability work. I did this intentionally and deliberately, to see what I could learn from working outside my comfort zone.

Some of the people with the most practice working on violence are deeply embedded within the criminal legal system or other punitive structures. I've had enlightening conversations about trends in homophobic and transphobic violence with prosecutors. I've also learned about de-escalating violence from bouncers and from school counselors. I deeply wanted to learn from people who had held down more incidents than I had.

This new experience expanded my knowledge and deepened my practice. I coordinated organizers in their efforts to implement advocacy and community-organizing strategies in response to more than 40 murders of queer and trans people.

I had the opportunity to refine my process, developing and presenting community-organizing options to recent survivors of violence and surviving family members. It was through this intense practice that I developed a process of rapid-response organizing in the aftermath of violence. I was able to use all the skills that I had developed while doing community safety campaigns and grow a deeper, more nuanced understanding of organizing around trauma. The ability to work with survivors of intimate partner violence, sexual violence, anti-LGBTQ violence and police violence was invaluable, as was my experience of working with survivors and organizers around the country.

I also want to acknowledge that in these times, taking time to practice can feel like a luxury. The urgency is real. We are dying. As a Black queer woman, I live and love in communities of survivors. But we will not create, implement and achieve the measured and nuanced community safety systems we deserve through shoddy and rushed attempts. Instead we will collectively weave our stories into strategies based on sharing what worked and what failed. So my question to you is: What has kept you alive so far? What are the lessons and themes and patterns that you can draw from? How can you practice safety? Where can you deepen your knowledge? And what unlikely allies can you recruit as learning partners?

Spending Less Time Judging Survivors

One day, while I was working at the Audre Lorde Project, I received an email that deeply upset me. We had recently attended a march organized by a mother whose gay son had been horrifically murdered. This mother had organized the march to raise awareness about her son's murder and was also passing out flyers that asked people to report information to the police. In response, I received this message from a critic:

"I can't believe that you would support state-based responses. Can you tell us about how this is in line with your politics?"

I was incensed by the email. While I didn't believe that the state would bring justice in this case, I believe in supporting Black mothers. I particularly believe in supporting Black mothers who are brave, proud and resilient enough to organize against homophobic violence in the face of devastating loss. I do not need to dictate or even believe in the strategies that surviving family members choose to use. Instead, I find ways to support them that are in line with my politics, because I know that just as punishment does not transform behavior, neither does judgment.

When we make judgment into one of our primary organizing strategies, we reduce the trust needed to create safety.

I know that when we say, "Don't call the cops!," we are usually envisioning that we're talking to privileged, college-educated, upper-class, mostly white people who aren't aware of the impact that calling the police has on communities of color. I also recognize that we need to push back against societal conditioning that tells us policing and prisons make us safer. Yet I believe that when people of color and particularly Black people make the choice to call emergency services, it is always a fraught decision. We have experienced state violence for generations. Many of us have family members in prison. Most of us have either directly experienced police violence or intimately know people who have. These are not flippant decisions. Yet when we create a culture of judgment so thick that we make it impossible for people to speak about the struggles they face when they call emergency services or need to, there are critical impacts. I've had many queer people of color, survivors or witnesses of violence, come to me for support, distraught that they had called 911.

"I heard my neighbor screaming. I couldn't figure out how to safely intervene. Was I wrong to call 911?"

When people who've experienced life-threatening injuries or people witnessing violence decide to call an ambulance, we must acknowledge that we have yet to build an alternative to 911. However, if we create a culture in which people feel comfortable sharing stories of the times when they called emergency services but didn't want to, we actually learn about crucial needs for community safety projects.

I believe that we can practice transformative justice while simultaneously reducing the harm from the state. Remembering that one of the primary goals of our work is relationship building, we must ask ourselves: Who wins when we shame survivors for using the only options available to them? The way forward lies in finding ways to balance compassion and critique, while also building our awareness of when to use which tool.

As a practical step, I would suggest examining when and why we use judgment in our conversations with each other and whether we're seeking to educate or support. We can reframe both education and support in nonjudgmental ways. For instance, education can include sharing tools for de-escalating conflict that a person can try to use before calling 911. We can achieve compassion without judgment when we focus on making sure that people feel heard, understood and not isolated. Compassionately discussing calling 911 with someone can sound like this: "I'm so sorry that happened. It seems like you didn't have very many options. If it's helpful, I'm happy to be someone you call on if you ever find yourself in that situation again."

In the end I'd like to offer these ideas as sparks for our collective imagination. To do this right, we must start small, build to scale, and allow ourselves to learn from both our successes and failures.

In this piece I have discussed smaller steps toward community safety, but in order to be successful, we must connect these strategies with larger liberatory movements. We must bring these ideas and conversations into our meetings, organizations and movements. We need to take time to include, within our demands and campaigns, strategies to build community safety and reduce harm. Even as we act urgently to resist the state violence that is killing our communities, we must also do slow work to develop community safety and resilience.

Acknowledgments

Creating an anthology is a deeply collective effort. Our thanks go first and foremost to the investigative journalists and hard-working activists whose incisive reports and bold political visions constitute the flesh and bones of this collection.

This book would not have been possible without the support of everyone on the Truthout team. Leslie Thatcher, our former content relations editor and a tireless part of Truthout's work for over a dozen years, commissioned and provided early edits to many of the pieces included in this book, and we are so grateful for her indispensable work. Jared Rodriguez supplied the idea and beautiful original image for the cover design. Truthout's staff, interns and fellows—including our beloved former managing editor Victoria Harper—played crucial roles in preparing the original versions of these articles for publication online and sharing them with readers far and wide.

Truthout would not exist as a platform for analyses such as these without the hundreds of contributing writers whose work appears on our site every year, nor without the dedicated readers who support us financially and by spreading the word about our journalistic work. Truthout's board of directors and board of advisers also supported the publication of these and other pieces by helping Truthout to thrive as a truly independent media site in a corporate-dominated media landscape.

We would also like to thank the Haymarket team, including Julie Fain, Anthony Arnove, Jim Plank, Rory Fanning, Rachel Cohen, and everyone else who made the process of putting out this collection far simpler than we could have hoped.

Finally, we would like to thank our political communities, friends and loved ones for their support during the creation of this anthology, with a special shoutout to Amanda Armstrong, Ryan Croken and Megan Groves.

About the Editors

 **Maya Schenwar** is Truthout's editor-in-chief. She is also the author of "Locked Down, Locked Out: Why Prison Doesn't Work and How We Can Do Better." Her work on the criminal legal system has been published on Truthout and in the New York Times, the Guardian, and the Nation, among others.

 **Joe Macaré** is Truthout's publisher. His interest in police repression began among the protesters, observers and bystanders "kettled" for seven hours by the London Metropolitan Police on May Day 2001. He has written for the Occupied Chicago Tribune, Red Wedge, In These Times, and various defunct British music publications.

 **Alana Yu-lan Price** is Truthout's content relations editor. She brings a deep commitment to racial justice, economic justice, and queer and trans liberation to her journalistic work. She previously served as managing editor of Tikkun magazine, which won two first-place awards from the Religion Newswriters Association under her leadership.

About the Contributors

William C. Anderson is a freelance writer and a contributing editor at Kalamazoo College's Praxis Center. He frequently writes news analysis and social commentary on a wide range of topics.

Candice Bernd is an editor and staff reporter at Truthout. Previously, she was an editor and reporter for Generation Progress, an intern at In These Times, and a co-host of a Dallas-based progressive radio program. With her partner, she co-wrote and produced "Don't Frack With Denton," a documentary chronicling how her hometown became the first in Texas to ban fracking.

Aaron Miguel Cantú is an investigative journalist and analyst focusing on the criminal justice system, national security and climate change politics. His work has been published in Truthout, Al Jazeera America, the Nation, the Intercept, and elsewhere. He was raised in the southern borderlands but is now based in Brooklyn.

Thandisizwe Chimurenga is currently a staff writer for Daily Kos and hosts a weekly news and public affairs show on the Pacifica Radio Network. She is the author of "No Doubt: The Murder(s) of Oscar Grant" (2014) and "Reparations … Not Yet" (2015). She is based in Los Angeles.

Ejeris Dixon is an organizer with 15 years of experience working in racial-justice, LGBTQ, transformative-justice, anti-violence, and economic-justice movements. She was the founding program coordinator of the S.O.S. Collective at the Audre Lorde

Project and now works as the founding director of Vision Change Win Consulting.

Alison Flowers is an award-winning journalist and author of "Exoneree Diaries: The Fight for Innocence, Independence and Identity." Her yearlong Chicago Public Media series was a finalist for a national Online Journalism Award in 2014. Flowers is a Social Justice News Nexus fellow and works at the Invisible Institute on the South Side of Chicago.

Alicia Garza is special projects director for the National Domestic Workers Alliance, co-creator of #BlackLivesMatter, organizer, writer, and freedom dreamer. She was named to The Root 100 2015 list of African-American achievers and influencers under 45, and The Politico 50 guide to thinkers, doers and visionaries transforming American politics in 2015.

Kelly Hayes is Truthout's community engagement associate. Kelly is a direct action trainer and a co-founder of The Chicago Light Brigade and Lifted Voices. She is the author of the blog Transformative Spaces, and her movement photography is featured in the "Freedom and Resistance" exhibit of the DuSable Museum of African American History.

Rachel Herzing is a co-founder of Critical Resistance, a national grassroots organization dedicated to abolishing the prison-industrial complex, and co-director of the StoryTelling & Organizing Project, a community resource for sharing stories of interventions in interpersonal harm that do not rely on policing, imprisonment or traditional social services.

Adam Hudson is a writer, journalist and musician based in the San Francisco Bay Area. He writes about US militarism, Guantánamo, policing and gentrification. His writings are published in Truthout, AlterNet, the Nation and elsewhere. He's the drummer for the alternative rock band Sunata and a Stanford University alumnus.

Victoria Law is the author of "Resistance Behind Bars: The Struggles of Incarcerated Women," editor of the zine Tenacious: Art and Writings by Women in Prison, and a proud parent. She has written extensively about the criminal justice system, particularly its impact on women, for Truthout and other news outlets.

Mike Ludwig is an investigative and social-justice reporter for Truthout, where he has worked since 2010. He lives in New Orleans.

Sarah Macaraeg, based in Chicago, is an independent journalist and fellow with New America Media and with Investigative Reporters and Editors. Her work has been published in the Guardian, VICE, and Truthout, and has been cited in Al Jazeera America, ColorLines, Crain's Chicago Business, Fusion, and Best American Essays. She is on Twitter at @seramak.

Page May is a Chicago-based organizer and abolitionist with We Charge Genocide, BYP100, and Assata's Daughters. She is one of the eight youth delegates who traveled to the United Nations and the lead author of the shadow report submitted to the UN Committee Against Torture.

Nicholas Powers is the author of "The Ground Below Zero: 9/11 to Burning Man, New Orleans to Darfur, Haiti to Occupy Wall Street," published by Upset Press. He is an associate professor of English at SUNY Old Westbury, and his writings have appeared in the Village Voice, Alternet, and the Indypendent.

Andrea Ritchie is a Black lesbian police-misconduct attorney and organizer who has engaged in extensive research, litigation and advocacy on the policing of women and LGBT people of color over the past two decades. She is co-author of "Say Her Name: Resisting Police Brutality Against Black Women" and "Queer (In)Justice."

Roberto Rodriguez, Ph.D., is an award-winning writer and associate professor at the University of Arizona's Mexican American Studies Department. The author of "Justice: A Question of Race" and "Our Sacred Maiz Is Our Mother," he is currently writing a memoir/testimonio, "Yolqui," on the topic of torture and political violence.

Asha Rosa is a Black queer writer, student, organizer, and member of Black Youth Project 100. She led a private prison divestment campaign on her college campus, presented to the UN on police violence in Chicago with the We Charge Genocide delegation, and is dedicated to movements for prison abolition.

Monica Trinidad is a movement artist and organizer. In November 2014, Monica was one of eight delegates to travel to the United Nations to deliver a report on police violence against youth of color in Chicago. She is the founder of Brown and Proud Press, and organizes with We Charge Genocide.

Eisa Nefertari Ulen is the author of "Crystelle Mourning," a novel described by the Washington Post as "a call for healing in the African American community from generations of hurt and neglect." She has contributed to Essence, the Washington Post, Ms., Health, Ebony, TheRoot.com, TheGrio.com and Truthout. See EisaUlen.com and find her on Twitter at @EisaUlen.

Notes

Foreword

1 See chapter 4 in this volume.
2 See John Arvanitis, "The U.S. Prisons Network: A Cheap Supply Chain With No Checks & Balances?," *CSRwire*, June 11, 2014, available at www.csrwire.com/blog/posts/1383-the-u-s-prisons-network-a-cheap-supply-chain-with-no-checks-balances.
3 Malcolm X Grassroots Movement, "Operation Ghetto Storm: 2012 Annual Report on the Extrajudicial Killings of 313 Black People by Police, Security Guards and Vigilantes," updated edition (October 2013), available at http://mxgm.org.

Introduction

1 Los Angeles Police Department, "The Origin of the LAPD Motto," available on the LAPD website, www.lapdonline.org.

Killing the Future

1 Originally published at *Truthout* on April 29, 2015.
2 "Is Ferguson Feeding on the Poor? City Disproportionately Stops, Charges and Fines People of Color," *Democracy Now!*, August 27, 2014, available at www.democracynow.org.
3 Martin Gilens and Benjamin I. Page, "Testing Theories of American Politics: Elites, Interest Groups, and Average Citizens," *Perspectives on Politics* 12, no. 3 (September 2014): 564–81, doi:10.1017/S1537592714001595.

Ring of Snitches

1   Originally published at *Truthout* on March 31, 2015. Original support-
    ing documents uncovered by Aaron Miguel Cantú and referenced in this
    chapter can be viewed in the online version of the article at www.truth-
    out.org.

2   Rob Warden, *The Snitch System: How Snitch Testimony Sent Randy Steidl
    and Other Innocent Americans to Death Row* (Chicago: Northwestern Uni-
    versity School of Law Center on Wrongful Convictions, 2004), available
    online at www.innocenceproject.org.

3   Alexandra Natapof, "Beyond Unreliable: How Snitches Contribute to
    Wrongful Convictions," *Golden Gate University Law Review* 37, no. 1
    (2006): 108, available online at http://digitalcommons.law.ggu.edu.

4   See www.innocenceproject.org/causes-wrongful-conviction/informants.

5   State of Illinois, "Report of the Governor's Commission on Capital Pun-
    ishment" (report published April 2002), available online at http://chicago-
    justice.org.

6   Bob Egelko, "Law Requires Corroboration of Cellmate's Testimony,"
    SFGate, August 1, 2011, available at www.sfgate.com.

7   Kevin Michael, "Jailhouse Snitch Testimony Is Backfiring in California,"
    Vice, March 18, 2015, available at www.vice.com.

8   American Civil Liberties Union, American Civil Liberties Union of
    Michigan, and Michigan Campaign for Justice, "Faces of Failing Public
    Defense Systems: Portraits of Michigan's Constitutional Crisis" (report
    published April 2011), available at www.aclu.org.

9   See The National Registry of Exonerations, a project of the University of
    Michigan Law School, www.law.umich.edu/special/exoneration.

10 "Police Officer Kills Wife, Self," *Lawrence Journal-World*, February 22,
    1999.

11 Paul Egan, "Attorney Grievance Official Says He Was Fired for Reporting
    Vicious E-mails," *Detroit Free Press*, July 30, 2014, available at http://ar-
    chive.freep.com.

12 Lacino Hamilton and L. C. DeVine, "Irrational System," *Confabulator*,
    September 13, 2013, available at http://nofrillnews.wordpress.com.

13 United States Department of Justice Civil Rights Division, "Investigation
    of the Ferguson Police Department" (report published March 4, 2015),
    available at www.justice.gov.

14 David Ashenfelter and Joe Swickard, "Detroit Cops Are Deadliest in
    U.S.," *Detroit Free Press*, May 15, 2000, archived by The Police Policy Stud-
    ies Council at www.theppsc.org.

15 Nick Bunkley, "Detroit Police Lab Is Closed after Audit Finds Serious
    Errors in Many Cases," *New York Times*, September 25, 2008.

16 Steve Neavling, David Ashenfelter, and Gina Damron, "Dangerous Debris,
    Evidence Left in Closed Detroit Police Crime Lab," *Detroit Free Press*,
    May 27, 2011, available at http://archive.freep.com.

Amid Shootings, Chicago Police Department Upholds Culture of Impunity

1   Originally published at *Truthout* on October 22, 2014. This investigative story was published more than a year before the launch of the Citizens Police Data Project by the Invisible Institute, an interactive database of police misconduct complaints. The database, when first published in 2015, contained more than 56,000 misconduct complaints for more than 8,500 Chicago police officers, whereas the 2014 *Truthout* story analyzed a subset of this disciplinary data, merging it with other meaningful dimensions, including known shootings and employee information on current officers. Read Alison Flowers's and Sarah Macaraeg's follow-up stories on the Chicago Police Department at www.truth-out.org.

2   We Charge Genocide, "Police Violence against Chicago's Youth of Color" (report prepared for the United Nations Committee Against Torture on the occasion of its review of the United States of America's Third Periodic Report to the Committee Against Torture, September 2014), available at http://report.wechargegenocide.org.

3   On October 28, the Fraternal Order of Police filed an injunction preventing the release of lists "containing information related to complaints lodged against officers covering the time period between January 1, 1967 to the present" to reporters at the *Chicago Sun-Times* and *Chicago Tribune* who requested them by way of the Freedom of Information Act.

4   See the report forms at http://directives.chicagopolice.org/forms/CPD-11.377.pdf. On October 30, 2014, Chicago police superintendent Garry McCarthy issued a new directive, General Order G03-02-05, changing the nature of Tactical Response Reports. It was issued sixteen business days after the authors' second FOIA request for TRR records pertaining to six specific officers, a specific date and location in 2010, and two specific dates and locations in 2011. The authors had initially requested a broader range of TRR records on September 25, 2014. Compliance with the Freedom of Information Act, 5 ILCS 140, requires response to a FOIA request within seven working days. The original TRR directive, Special Order S03-02-01 ("Firearm Discharge Incidents Other than Incidents Involving the Destruction of an Animal"), was put in place to "outline Department investigative and reporting procedures in firearm discharge incidents." General Order G03-02-05, "Incidents Requiring the Completion of a Tactical Response Report," broadens the use of TRRs to include "incidents which involve a subject fitting the definition of an assailant ... the definition of an active resister ... [or] the definition of a passive resister," "incidents involving the discharge of OC spray or other chemical weapon, a Taser, impact munitions, or a firearm," and "incidents where a subject obstructs a police officer." The directive can be viewed online at http://directives.chicagopolice.org.

5   For this investigation, *Truthout* used Kalven's repeater list, among other public data.

6   Steve Schmadeke and Jeremy Gorner, "Anger Follows Acquittal in Rare Trial of Chicago Cop," *Chicago Tribune*, April 21, 2015.

7   "Dash Cam Video of Police Shooting," police surveillance video published online by the *Chicago Tribune*, n.d., www.chicagotribune.com/videos/chi-111020-surveillance-sierra-video-premiumvideo.html.

8   The following additional police shooters emerged in the investigation. They did not respond to requests from *Truthout* for comment: Officer Rick Caballero shot Ben Romaine, who was driving away from Caballero, and killed him; he was later awarded the Superintendent's Award for Valor for the incident, which settled in a civil suit. Officer Robert Haile shot and killed Lazuanjo Brooks multiple times and in the back; the shooting settled in a civil suit. Sergeant David Rodriguez shot Herbert Becker at close range; the shooting settled in a civil suit. Officer Vilma Argueta shot and killed nineteen-year-old George Lash on the Chicago Transit Authority; he received an award for the incident, which was voluntarily dismissed by the Lash family lawyers in a civil suit. Officer Darren Wright shot seventeen-year-old Corey Harris in the back and killed him; the shooting settled in a civil suit. Officers Shawn Lawryn and Juan Martinez shot and killed Esau Castellanos; in a civil suit currently underway, the complaint highlights ballistics reports contradicting the officers' accounts. Officer Michael St. Clair shot William Hope multiple times in the chest in broad daylight, while Hope was sitting in his car; the shooting later settled.

9   Wesley Lowery, "How Many Police Shootings a Year? No One Knows," *Washington Post*, September 8, 2014.

10   See www.fatalencounters.org.

Beyond Homan Square

1   Originally published at *Truthout* on March 26, 2015.

2   Spencer Ackerman, "The Disappeared: Chicago Police Detain Americans at Abuse-Laden 'Black Site,'" *Guardian*, February 24, 2015.

3   Ibid.

4   Ibid.

5   Ibid.

6   Ibid.

7   See, for example, Sven Beckert and Seth Rockman, "How Slavery Led to Modern Capitalism: Echoes," *BloombergView*, January 24, 2012, available at www.bloombergview.com.

8   See Noah Berlatsky, "America Is Built on Torture, Remember?," *Pacific Standard*, December 12, 2014, available at www.psmag.com.

9   Edward E. Baptist, The Half Has Never Been Told: Slavery and the Making of American Capitalism (New York: Basic Books, 2014), 141.

10   Sally E. Hadden and New Georgia Encyclopedia staff, "Slave Patrols," *New Georgia Encyclopedia*, last edited October 2014, available at www.

georgiaencyclopedia.org. See also Austin Steward, *Twenty-Two Years a Slave, and Forty Years a Freeman* (Rochester, NY: William Alling, 1857), excerpted in "The Making of African American Identity: Vol. I, 1500-1865," National Humanities Center Toolbox Library: Primary Resources in U.S. History & Literature, available at http://nationalhumanitiescenter. org.

11   Gloria J. Browne-Marshall, "Stop and Frisk: From Slave-Catchers to NYPD, A Legal Commentary," *Trotter Review* 21, no. 1 (2013), available at http://scholarworks.umb.edu/trotter_review.

12   Auandaru Nirhani, "Policing Slaves since the 1600s: White Supremacy, Slavery, and Modern US Police Departments," *Rebel Press*, January 7, 2012, http://therebelpress.com/articles/show?id=2.

13   See Gary Potter, *The History of Policing in the United States*, Eastern Kentucky University Police Studies Online, 2013, http://plsonline.eku.edu/ insidelook/history-policing-united-states-part-1. See also David White-house, "Origins of the Police," *Works in Theory* (blog), December 7, 2014, available at http://worxintheory.wordpress.com.

14   Victor E. Kappeler, "A Brief History of Slavery and the Origins of American Policing," Eastern Kentucky University Police Studies Online, January 7, 2014, http://plsonline.eku.edu/insidelook/brief-history-slavery-and-origins-american-policing.

15   Paul Kramer, "The Water Cure," *New Yorker*, February 25, 2008.

16   United Nations Committee against Torture, "Concluding Observations on the Third to Fifth Periodic Reports of United States of America" (advance unedited version, November 20, 2014), website of the Office of the United Nations High Commissioner for Human Rights, http://tbinternet.ohchr. org/Treaties/CAT/Shared%20Documents/USA/INT_CAT_COC_US-A_18893_E.pdf. The full United Nations "Convention against Torture and Other Cruel, Inhuman or Degrading Treatment or Punishment" is also available at www.ohchr.org.

17   See Chapter 11 for more information.

18   Alfred de Zayas, "Human Rights and Indefinite Detention," *International Review of the Red Cross* 87, no. 857 (March 2005), available at www.icrc. org. For the full United Nations "International Covenant on Civil and Political Rights," see www.ohchr.org.

19   Guatemala Acupuncture and Medical Aid Project, "Deprivation, Not Deterrence" (report published October 2014), available at www.document-cloud.org/documents/1377704-544f3e9ad7ba4-1.html.

20   Ed Pilkington, "Freezing Cells and Sleep Deprivation: The Brutal Conditions Migrants Still Face after Capture," *Guardian*, December 12, 2014.

21   American Civil Liberties Union, "End the Overuse of Solitary Confinement" (fact sheet, posted on the ACLU website June 6, 2013), available at www.aclu.org/stop-solitary-two-pager.

22   Solitary Watch, "FAQ," http://solitarywatch.com/facts/faq.

23   George Dvorsky, "Why Solitary Confinement Is the Worst Kind of Psy-

chological Torture," *io9*, July 1, 2014, available at http://io9.com.

24   Solitary Watch, "FAQ."

25   See "The Istanbul Statement on the Use and Effects of Solitary Confinement" (statement adopted on December 9, 2007, by the International Psychological Trauma Symposium, Istanbul) and "Interim Report of the Special Rapporteur of the Human Rights Council on Torture and Other Cruel, Inhuman or Degrading Treatment or Punishment" (report submitted to the UN General Assembly, August 5, 2011), both available at http://solitaryconfinement.org. See also Human Rights Watch, "US: Look Critically at Widespread Use of Solitary Confinement" (statement to the US Senate Committee on the Judiciary, Subcommittee on the Constitution, Civil Rights, and Human Rights, June 18, 2012), available at www.hrw.org, and Jules Lobel, "Prolonged Solitary Confinement and the Constitution," *Journal of Constitutional Law* 11, no. 1 (December 2008), available at www.law.upenn.edu/journals.

26   Malcolm X Grassroots Movement, "Operation Ghetto Storm: 2012 Annual Report on the Extrajudicial Killings of 313 Black People by Police, Security Guards and Vigilantes," updated edition (October 2013), available at http://mxgm.org.

27   Kevin Johnson, Meghan Hoyer, and Brad Heath, "Local Police Involved in 400 Killings per Year," *USA Today*, August 15, 2014.

28   See chapter 11.

29   In addition to chapter 11, see A. Pulley, "Chicago Activists 'Charge Genocide' at United Nations," *Ebony*, November 17, 2014, and We Charge Genocide, "We Charge Genocide Sends Delegation to United Nations" (summary report, December 15, 2014), available at http://wechargegenocide.org.

30   We Charge Genocide, "Police Violence against Chicago's Youth of Color" (report prepared for the United Nations Committee Against Torture on the occasion of its review of the United States of America's Third Periodic Report to the Committee Against Torture, September 2014), available at http://report.wechargegenocide.org.

31   Adam Hudson, "Libya and Somalia Raids—More Rendition, More Wars in Africa," *Free Your Mind* (blog), November 1, 2013, available at http://adamhudson.org.

32   Jomana Karadsheh, "Alleged al Qaeda Operative Abu Anas al Libi Dies in U.S. Hospital, Family Says," CNN website, January 3, 2015.

33   Joshua Keating, "Is the U.S. Leaving Itself Wiggle Room on Torture?," *Slate*, November 14, 2014.

34   Charlie Savage, "U.S. to Revise Bush Policy on Treatment of Prisoners," *New York Times*, November 12, 2014.

35   Matthieu Aikins, "The A-Team Killings," *Rolling Stone*, November 6, 2013.

36   Matthieu Aikins, "Watch Highly Disturbing Footage of Detainee Abuses in Afghanistan," *Rolling Stone*, November 7, 2013.

37   Ibid.

38   Phil Stewart and Emily Stephenson, "U.S. to Fund Afghan Forces at Peak Level through 2017: Officials," Reuters, March 23, 2015.

39   Rod Nordland and Taimoor Shah, "Afghanistan Quietly Lifts Ban on Nighttime Raids," *New York Times*, November 23, 2014.

40   "Obama's Lists: A Dubious History of Targeted Killings in Afghanistan," *Spiegel Online*, December 28, 2014.

41   Jeremy Scahill, "The CIA's Secret Sites in Somalia," *Nation*, December 10, 2014.

42   Ibid.

43   Cora Currier, "CIA Director Describes How the U.S. Outsources Terror Interrogations," *Intercept*, March 13, 2015, available at http://theintercept.com.

44   John O. Brennan, "U.S. Intelligence in a Transforming World" (speech to the Council on Foreign Relations, March 13, 2015), available at www.cfr.org.

"Never Again a World Without Us"

1   Originally published at *Truthout* on February 4, 2015. Sources for this chapter as a whole include W. D. Carrigan and C. Webb, *Forgotten Dead: Mob Violence against Mexicans in the United States, 1848–1928* (Oxford: Oxford University Press, 2013); R. Bauman, review of Lauren Araiza, *To March for Others: The Black Freedom Struggle and the United Farm Workers*, *American Historical Review* 119, no. 5 (December 2014): 1724–25; R. Delgado, "The Law of the Noose: A History of Latino Lynching," *Harvard Civil Rights-Civil Liberties Law Review* 44, no. 2 (Summer 2009): 297; E. J. Escobar, *Race, Police, and the Making of a Political Identity: Mexican Americans and the Los Angeles Police Department, 1900–1945* (Berkeley: University of California Press, 1999); Domingo Martínez Paredez, "Un continente y una cultura," in *Unidad filológica de la América prehispana* (México: Poesía de América, 1960); A. Morales, *Ando Sangrando (I Am Bleeding): A Study of Mexican American-Police Conflict* (La Puente, CA: Perspectiva Publications, 1972): 100–107; S. T. Newcomb, *Pagans in the Promised Land: Decoding the Doctrine of Christian Discovery* (Golden, CO: Fulcrum Publishing, 2008); R. Rodríguez, *Assault with a Deadly Weapon: About an Incident in ELA and the Closing of Whittier Boulevard* (Los Angeles: Libreria Latinoamericana, 1984); R. Rodríguez, *Justice: A Question of Race* (Phoenix: Bilingual Review Press, 1997).

2   Roberto Rodriguez, "Commemorating Victories," *Truthout*, November 21, 2009.

3   *American Experience*, "Zoot Suit Riots," Season 14 Episode 10, written and directed by Joseph Tovares, PBS, March 1, 2002.

4   Roberto Rodriguez, "Pachuco Yo, Ese," *Lowrider* 2, no. 4 (1978).

5   Cecilia Rasmussen, "The 'Bloody Christmas' of 1951," *Los Angeles Times*, December 21, 1997.

6   Patrisia Gonzales and Roberto Rodriguez, "$4,000: The Price of a Mexi-

can," ¡LatinoLA!, August 31, 2001, available at http://latinola.com.

7   Julia Preston, "Beating Increases Tension on Immigration," *New York Times*, April 6, 1996; Roberto Rodriguez, "Beyond Brutality: Scholars Say Repeated Beatings Born in Hate and Police Culture," *Diverse: Issues in Higher Education*, June 18, 2007, available at http://diverseeducation.com.

8   "Force at the Border," *Arizona Republic*, March 25, 2014, available at www.azcentral.com.

9   Tim Johnson, "Questions Still Unanswered about U.S. Border Patrol's Killing of 16-Year-Old," *McClatchyDC*, March 21, 2014, www.mcclatchy-dc.com/news/crime/article24765517.html.

10   Jesse Paul and Noelle Phillips, "Denver Police Fatally Shoot Teen Girl Suspect; Officer Hit by Car," *Denver Post*, January 26, 2014, available at www.denverpost.com.

11   R. Stickney and Wendy Fry, "Man Dies in Custody at U.S. Border Crossing," NBC 7 San Diego, December 25, 2014, available at www.nbcsandiego.com.

12   Christie Locke and Darrell Locke, "Family Statement: Lakota Man Shot by Rapid City Police after Native Lives Matter Rally," *Censored News* (blog), December 22, 2014, available at http://bsnorrell.blogspot.com.

13   Matt Remle, "Six Native Americans Killed by Police in Last Two Months of 2014," *Last Real Indians*, available at http://lastrealindians.com.

14   Betson08, "Skinheads Hunt Native American Family: Guess Who Gets Arrested?," *Daily Kos*, July 10, 2011.

15   Abby Phillip, "Texas Cop Uses a Stun Gun on a 76-Year-Old Driver He Pulled Over for a Nonexistent Inspection Violation," *Washington Post*, December 15, 2014.

16   "2 Killed in East LA Deputy Involved Shooting," CBS Los Angeles, November 16, 2014, available at http://losangeles.cbslocal.com.

17   "Family Of Man Fatally Shot By LA County Sheriff's Department Files Damages Claim," CBS Los Angeles, December 19, 2014, available at http://losangeles.cbslocal.com.

18   Walter Einenkel, "Denver Police Erase Video Evidence of Them Flipping 7-Month-Pregnant Woman and Pummeling Her Friend," *Daily Kos*, December 3, 2014.

19   Kate Mather, Richard Winton, and Cindy Chang, "Ezell Ford Autopsy, LAPD Chief Disclose New Details of Shooting," *Los Angeles Times*, December 29, 2013.

20   Tracy Bloom and Nerissa Knight, "Man Dies after Violent Altercation with LAPD Officers a Week before Ezell Ford Shooting, Family Says," KTLA 5, August 14, 2014, available at http://ktla.com.

21   Matthew Brown, "Killing of Unarmed Montana Man by Police Found Justified," Associated Press, January 7, 2015, available at http://news.yahoo.com.

22   Carl Finamore, "'Why Did Police Kill Our Son?,'" *CounterPunch*, December 5, 2014, available at www.counterpunch.org.

23 "Police Beat Father to Death in Front of His Wife and Daughter, Steal Daughter's Camera Afterwards," Filming Cops, last updated February 25, 2014, available at http://filmingcops.com.

24 Mark Matthews, NBC Bay Area staff, and wire services, "No Charges in Shooting of 13-Year-Old Andy Lopez by Sonoma County Sheriff's Deputy," NBC Bay Area, July 8, 2014, available at www.nbcbayarea.com.

25 Andalusia Knoll, "We Want Them Alive: The Search for Mexico's 43 Missing Students," *Waging Nonviolence*, October 21, 2014, available at http://wagingnonviolence.org.

26 Human Rights Watch, "World Report 2014," available at www.hrw.org.

27 See "*Walkout*: The True Story of the Historic 1968 Chicano Student Walkout in East L.A.," *Democracy Now!*, March 29, 2006, available at www.democracynow.org.

28 Eric Struch, "Puerto Ricans Rebelled against Police Violence," *Workers World*, July 3, 2006, available at www.workers.org.

29 Dianne Solis, "40 Years after Santos Rodriguez's Murder, Scars Remain for Family, Neighbors and Dallas," *Dallas Morning News*, July 21, 2013, available at www.dallasnews.com.

30 Thaddeus Herrick, "Borderline Shootings: Two Cases This Year Raise Questions about Military's Role on Rio Grande," *Houston Chronicle*, June 22, 1997, archived at www.dpft.org/hernandez/chronicle_june_22.html.

31 Nicole Flatow, "The United States Has the Largest Prison Population in the World—And It's Growing," *ThinkProgress*, September 17, 2014, available at http://thinkprogress.org.

32 Victoria Bekiempis, "Report: Half of Federal Arrests Are on Immigration Charges," *Newsweek*, January 24, 2015.

33 Brian Charles and Paul Penzella, "Southern California Gang Injunctions," *Long Beach Press-Telegram* video, September 2013, www.presstelegram.com/gang-injunctions.

34 United States Department of Justice, "Guidance for Federal Law Enforcement Agencies regarding the Use of Race, Ethnicity, Gender, National Origin, Religion, Sexual Orientation, or Gender Identity" (December 2014), available at www.justice.gov.

35 Esther Yu-Hsi Lee, "How the Postville Immigration Raid Has Changed Deportation Proceedings," *ThinkProgress*, May 10, 2013, available at http://thinkprogress.org.

36 S. T. McNeil, "Streamlined Deportation: 'No One Here in This Room Can Help You,'" *Truthout*, January 3, 2013.

37 "Operation Streamline: Expedited Indian Removal," *Truthout*, October 9, 2013.

Killing Africa

1 Originally published at *Truthout* on April 17, 2015.

2   Gale Holland, "Dozens Protest LAPD Shooting of Homeless Man on Skid Row," *Los Angeles Times*, March 7, 2015.

3   For further commentary, see William C. Anderson, "From Lynching Photos to Michael Brown's Body: Commodifying Black Death," *Truthout*, January 16, 2015.

4   Lauren Gambino, "Homeless Man Shot Dead by LAPD Was Not Deported Due to Stolen Identity," *Guardian*, March 4, 2015.

5   United Nations Development Programme, "Economic Growth Alone Not Enough to Face Africa's Emerging Challenges, UN Development Chief" (press release, March 18, 2015), available at www.undp.org.

6   United Nations Meetings Coverage and Press Releases, "'Intervention Brigade' Authorized as Security Council Grants Mandate Renewal for United Nations Mission in Democratic Republic of Congo" (meeting coverage, March 28, 2013), available at www.un.org/press.

7   UN News Service, "DR Congo: UN Peacekeeping on Offensive after Defeat of M23, Says Senior UN Official," *UN News Centre*, December 11, 2013, www.un.org/apps/news/story.asp?newsid=46721#.VhM9FrRViko.

8   Cara Anna, "UN Waived Human Rights Concerns over 2 Congo Generals," Associated Press, March 19, 2015, www.washingtontimes.com/news/2015/mar/19/congo-pushes-back-against-un-peacekeeping-force-cu.

9   Ed Pilkington, "Haitians Launch New Lawsuit against UN over Thousands of Cholera Deaths," *Guardian*, March 11, 2014.

10   Richard Knox, "Activists Sue U.N. over Cholera That Killed Thousands in Haiti," NPR, October 9, 2013.

11   "UN 'Immune' from Haiti Cholera Lawsuit," *Al Jazeera*, January 10, 2015.

12   Abraham Paulos, "U.S. Criminal Deportations and the Future of Black Immigrants," *Huffington Post*, February 26, 2015.

13   Nancy Porsia and Chris Stephen, "Eritrean Migrants Risk Detentions and Beatings in Libya for a Life in Europe," *Guardian*, August 1, 2014.

14   John Hooper, Patrick Kingsley, and Ben Quinn, "Smugglers Abandon Migrant Ship off Italy in New Tactic to Force Rescue," *Guardian*, January 2, 2015.

15   "African Migrants in Israel's Holot Detention Centre," *Guardian* video, December 19, 2014.

16   Lewis Dean, "Revealed: Dangerous Routes African Migrants Use to Reach UK," *International Business Times*, March 19, 2015.

17   "Yemeni Refugees Fleeing Conflict Arrive in Somalia, UNHCR," *Mareeg.com*, March 30, 2015, available at www.mareeg.com.

18   Mark Anderson, "Norway Minister Threatens to Deport Eritrean Migrants," *Guardian*, June 27, 2014.

19   Jibril Adan, "Kenya, China Partnership to Focus on Industrialisation," *allAfrica*, January 10, 2015, http://allafrica.com/stories/201501110109.html.

20   Murithi Mutiga, "Are the Terrorists of al-Shabaab about to Tear Kenya in Two?," *Observer*, April 4, 2015, available at www.theguardian.com.

21   Brian Ries, "Police Tear Gas Kids Protesting Removal of Their Play-

ground," *Mashable*, January 19, 2015, available at http://mashable.com.

22   Pete Pattisson, "Women from Sierra Leone 'Sold like Slaves' into Domestic Work in Kuwait," *Guardian*, April 2, 2015.

23   Human Rights Watch, "Ethiopia: Forced Relocations Bring Hunger, Hardship," January 16, 2012, available at www.hrw.org.

24   Helene Cooper and Eric Schmitt, "U.S. Targets Shabab Unit in Somalia," *New York Times*, March 13, 2015.

25   Adam Rawnsley, "It Seems a Chinese Missile Drone Just Crashed in Nigeria," *Medium*, January 28, 2015, available at http://medium.com.

26   Nick Turse, "The Pivot to Africa: The Startling Size, Scope, and Growth of U.S. Military Operations on the African Continent," *TomDispatch*, September 5, 2013, www.tomdispatch.com/post/175743.

27   Helene Cooper, Michael D. Shear, and Denise Grady, "U.S. to Commit up to 3,000 Troops to Fight Ebola in Africa," *New York Times*, September 15, 2014.

28   Adam Taylor, "MAP: The U.S. Military Currently Has Troops in These African Countries," *Washington Post*, May 21, 2014.

29   Murithi Mutiga, "'No Africans' Chinese Restaurant Owner Arrested in Nairobi," *Guardian*, March 24, 2015.

30   Randeep Ramesh, "More Black People Jailed in England and Wales Proportionally than in US," *Guardian*, October 10, 2010.

31   Ibid.

32   Mark Townsend, "No Convictions over 500 Black and Asian Deaths in Custody," *Guardian*, March 21, 2015.

33   Ibid.

34   Significant contributions to the perspective mentioned in reference to the man called Africa came from conversations with a close friend of his who didn't wish to be mentioned. This friend, who also knew him as "Both" (a name he gained at a halfway house because he spoke about things in twos), spent significant amounts of time around him. Africa's friend spoke of him in the highest regard and shared many stories of the good things people had to say about him. Africa's friend also shared that he was an aspiring writer who had completed at least two books and hoped to have a career in Hollywood. It's my hope that my telling of his story lives up to any standards of writing he may have had for his own work. Rest in peace, Africa.

35   "We are here alive today because our ancestors dared to dream / From Africa they lay in the bilge of slave ships / And stood half naked on auction blocks / From Eastern Europe they crowded in vessels overloaded with immigrants / And were mis-named on Ellis Island." Poem written for Common, *The Dreamer / The Believer*, with Maya Angelou, Lonnie Lynn, James Fauntleroy II, and Ernest Wilson (Warner Bros. Records, 2011).

Say Her Name

1   Originally published at *Truthout*, September 18, 2015.

2   David Montgomery, "Sandra Bland Was Threatened with Taser, Police Video Shows," *New York Times*, July 21, 2015.

3   Ray Sanchez, "What We Know about the Controversy in Sandra Bland's Death," CNN website, July 22, 2015.

4   AJ+, "Sandra Bland Found Dead in Texas Jail Cell" (video, Al Jazeera multimedia channel AJ+, July 16, 2015), www.youtube.com/watch?v=-rEN-6OXFws.

5   K. K. Rebecca Lai, Haeyoun Park, Larry Buchanan, and Wilson Andrews, "Assessing the Legality of Sandra Bland's Arrest," *New York Times*, July 22, 2015.

6   Evan Seymour, "In Her Own Words: The Haunting Importance of Sandra Bland's 'Sandy Speaks' Videos," *For Harriet*, July 20, 2015, available at www.forharriet.com.

7   Sophia Bollag, "Locals Hold Vigil, Grapple with Sandra Bland's Death," *Texas Tribune*, July 18, 2015, available at www.texastribune.org.

8   Breanna Edwards, "At Least 5 Black Women Have Died in Police Custody in July; WTF?!," *The Root*, July 30, 2015, available at www.theroot.com.

9   Moreh B. D. K., "The 'Female Eric Garner' Who Suffocated to Death in Police Custody," *Counter Current News*, December 27, 2014, http://countercurrentnews.com/2014/12/sheneque-proctor-the-female-eric-garner.

10   Jane Janeczko, "Kyam Livingston's Family Sues NYPD after Death in Holding Cell," *Huffington Post*, October 23, 2013.

11   Carimah Townes, "No Criminal Charges for Deputies Who Tased Shackled Woman with Four 50,000 Volt Shocks," *ThinkProgress*, September 9, 2015, available at http://thinkprogress.org.

12   R. Lundman and R. Kaufman, "Driving while Black: Effects of Race, Ethnicity, and Gender on Citizen Reports of Traffic Stops and Police Action," *Criminology* 41, no. 1 (February 2003): 195.

13   Office of the Missouri Attorney General, "Racial Profiling Data 2013," Office of the Missouri Attorney General website, http://ago.mo.gov/docs/default-source/public-safety/2013agencyreports.pdf.

14   Kathryn K. Russell, *The Color of Crime: Racial Hoaxes, White Fear, Black Protectionism, Police Harassment, and Other Macroaggressions* (New York: NYU Press, 1999), 36; "Dr. Mae Jemison Was Made to Walk Barefoot," *New York Amsterdam News* 87, no. 11 (March 16, 1996): 4.

15   Michael Zennie and Alex Greig, "Pictured: The Two Women Suing Police after They Were Subjected to Humiliating Roadside Cavity Search as They Wore Only Their Bikinis," *Daily Mail*, July 5, 2013, available at www.dailymail.co.uk.

16   Jacob Sullum, "The War on Drugs Now Features Roadside Sexual Assaults by Cops," *Forbes*, May 7, 2015.

17   Solutions Not Punishment Coalition, "Victory! East Point Police Department to Adopt Most Progressive Trans Policies in the Nation" (press

release, Racial Justice Action Center, April 9, 2015), www.rjactioncenter. org/EastPointVictory.

18 See Andrea J. Ritchie, "Law Enforcement Violence against Women of Color," in *Color of Violence: The Incite! Anthology* (Brooklyn, NY: South End Press, 2006).

19 Todd Lighty, "Untold Story of Haggerty Shooting," *Chicago Tribune*, September 12, 1999.

20 Maxine Bernstein, "Memorial Planned to Mark 10-Year Anniversary of Portland Police Fatal Shooting of Kendra James," *Oregonian*, April 29, 2013, available at www.oregonlive.com.

21 Ida Lieszkovszky, "Everything You Need to Know before the Start of the Trial for Cleveland Police Officer Michael Brelo," *Cleveland.com*, April 6, 2015, available at www.cleveland.com.

22 Peter Hermann, "Baltimore's Transgender Community Mourns One of Their Own, Slain by Police," *Washington Post*, April 3, 2015.

23 Jessica Testa, "How Police Caught the Cop Who Allegedly Sexually Abused 8 Black Women," *BuzzFeed*, September 5, 2014, available at www. buzzfeed.com.

24 International Association of Chiefs of Police, *Addressing Sexual Offenses and Misconduct by Law Enforcement: Executive Guide* (June 2011), available at www.theiacp.org.

25 The Cato Institute's National Police Misconduct Reporting Project, "2010 Annual Report," available at www.policemisconduct.net.

26 Dylan Stableford, "Bikini-Clad Girl Thrown to Ground by McKinney Officer Speaks Out," *Yahoo News*, June 8, 2015, available at http://news. yahoo.com.

27 Fred Clasen-Kelly, "Witness: Officer Didn't Have to Shoot," *Charlotte Observer*, February 20, 2015, www.charlotteobserver.com/news/local/crime/ article10783382.html.

28 See Ritchie, "Law Enforcement Violence against Women of Color."

29 National Coalition of Anti-Violence Programs, "NCAVP Mourns the Killing of Queer Youth of Color Jessie Hernandez; Calls for National Awareness on Police Violence Facing LGBTQ People of Color" (press release, January 30, 2015), available at http://coavp.org.

30 Kimberle Williams Crenshaw and Andrea J. Ritchie, "Say Her Name: Resisting Police Brutality against Black Women" (report published by the African American Policy Forum and the Center for Intersectionality and Social Policy Studies of Columbia Law School, May 2015; updated July 2015), available at www.aapf.org.

31 Women's Prison Association, "Quick Facts: Women & Criminal Justice—2009" (fact sheet, September 2009), available at www.wpaonline.org.

32 Shana M. Judge and Mariah Wood, "Racial Disparities in the Enforcement of Prostitution Laws" (panel presentation at the Global Challenges, New Perspectives conference, Association for Public Policy Analysis and Management, November 6, 2014), http://appam.confex.com/appam/2014/

webprogram/Paper11163.html.

33   Alicia Garza, "A Herstory of the #BlackLivesMatter Movement by Alicia Garza," *Feminist Wire*, October 7, 2014, available at www.thefeministwire. com.

34   See http://byp100.org/justice-for-rekia.

35   Ashoka Jegroo, "Across the US, Activists Shine Light on Sandra Bland's Mysterious Death," *Waging Nonviolence*, July 30, 2015, available at http:// wagingnonviolence.org.

36   The exhibit "Blood at the Root: Unearthing the Stories of State Violence against Black Women," the curators of which included Mariame Kaba, Rachel Caidor, and Ayanna Banks Harris, ran from August to October 2014 at Chicago's Holy Covenant United Methodist Church. See Kate Shepherd, "Black Women Brutalized by Cops Are Subject of New Lincoln Park Exhibit," *Chicagoist*, August 18, 2015, available at http://chicagoist. com.

37   Office of United States Congressman John Conyers Jr., "Summary of the End Racial Profiling Act of 2015," April 22, 2015 (accessed at http:// conyers.house.gov; file is no longer online).

38   For insight into why this is necessary, see the NAACP report "Born Suspect: Stop-and-Frisk Abuses & the Continued Fight to End Racial Profiling in America" (September 2014), available at http://action.naacp. org.

39   President's Task Force on 21st Century Policing, "Final Report of the President's Task Force on 21st Century Policing" (report published by the Office of Community Oriented Policing Services, 2015), available at www. cops.usdoj.gov.

40   Andrea J. Ritchie, "Policy and Oversight: Women of Color's Experiences of Policing" (report submitted to the President's Task Force on 21st Century Policing, January 28, 2015), http://changethenypd.org.

Your Pregnancy May Subject You to Even More Law Enforcement Violence

1   Originally published at *Truthout* on April 23, 2015.

2   El Grito de Sunset Park, "NYPD 72nd Pct. Officers Slam Pregnant Woman onto Street" (video posted to El Grito de Sunset Park Facebook page, September 23, 2014), www.facebook.com/video.php?v=660936530680965.

3   Elle Griffiths, "Jeanetta Riley: Shocking Video Shows Cops Shooting Dead 'Mentally Ill' Pregnant Woman as She Brandishes Knife," *Daily Mirror*, April 6, 2015, available at www.mirror.co.uk.

4   Julia Preston, "Immigrant, Pregnant, Is Jailed under Pact," *New York Times*, July 20, 2008.

5   Amy Martyn, "A Texas Inmate's Newborn Died after She Gave Birth in Solitary Confinement, Lawsuit Claims," *Dallas Observer*, June 27, 2014,

available at www.dallasobserver.com.

6   Diana Claitor and Burke Butler, "Pregnant Women in Texas County Jails
     Deserve Better than This," *Dallas Morning News*, June 26, 2014, www.
     dallasnews.com/opinion/latest-columns/20140626-pregnant-women-in-
     texas-county-jails-deserve-better-than-this.ece.

7   Anonymous, "Shackled on Rikers Island during an Ectopic Pregnancy,"
     Birthing Behind Bars, March 6, 2014, available at http://nationinside.org.

8   See http://docs.legis.wisconsin.gov/statutes/statutes/48/III/133.

9   National Conference of State Legislatures, "Fetal Homicide State Laws"
     (online resource, March 2015), available at www.ncsl.org.

10   *Brief of Amicus Curiae: Postpartum Support International, Dr. Vivien K. Burt,
     Professor Michelle Oberman and Dr. Margaret Spinelli on Perinatal Psychi-
     atric Illness in Support of Appellant's Petition to Transfer*, State of Indiana v.
     Bei Bei Shuai, filed March 9, 2012, http://advocatesforpregnantwomen.
     org/2012-03-09%20-%20Shuai%20-%20Brief%20of%20Amicus%20Cur-
     iae%20of%20Postpartum%20Support%20International%20et%20al%20
     -%20Cantor_Foste.PDF.

11   Anna Halkidis, "Bei Bei Shuai Case Exposes Pregnancy-Suicide Risk,"
     WeNews, August 7, 2013, available at http://womensenews.org.

12   Farah Diaz-Tello and Laura Huss, "It Is All Too Easy for Pregnant Wom-
     en to Be Put on Trial in the United States," *RH Reality Check*, March 30,
     2015, http://rhrealitycheck.org/article/2015/03/30/easy-pregnant-women-
     put-trial-united-states.

13   Kathy Bouger, "Report: 'Scientific' Test Used to Convict Women in El
     Salvador Is Anything But," *RH Reality Check*, October 17, 2014, http://
     rhrealitycheck.org/article/2014/10/17/report-scientific-test-used-con-
     vict-women-el-salvador-anything.

14   Emily Bazelon, "Purvi Patel Could Be Just the Beginning," *New York
     Times Magazine*, April 1, 2015.

15   Alyssa Johnston, "Lawsuit: Inmate in Solitary Confinement Says Jail
     Ignored Birth, Leading to Baby's Death," *Independent Mail*, May 23, 2014,
     available at www.independentmail.com.

16   See http://codes.lp.findlaw.com/alcode/26/15/26-15-3.2.

17   National Advocates for Pregnant Women, "Pregnant Woman Files Civil
     Rights Lawsuit against State of Wisconsin Challenging Wisconsin Law
     That Permits Jailing" (press release, December 16, 2014), available at
     http://advocatesforpregnantwomen.org.

Black Parenting Matters

1   Originally posted at *Truthout* on October 1, 2015.

2   See "The Middle Passage," in "The Terrible Transformation: 1450–1750,"
     Africans in America Resource Bank, PBS, available at www.pbs.org/wgbh/
     aia/home.html.

3   Brendan Wolfe, "Slavery by the Numbers," Encyclopedia Virginia blog, December 1, 2011, available at http://blog.encyclopediavirginia.org.

4   Robert A. Gibson, "The Negro Holocaust: Lynching and Race Riots in the United States,1880–1950," Yale–New Haven Teachers Institute Curriculum Units (1979, volume 2), available at http://www.yale.edu/ynhti/curriculum/units/1979/2.

5   Tuskegee Institute statistics. See http://law2.umkc.edu/faculty/projects/ftrials/shipp/lynchingyear.html.

6   Kimberly Kindy, Julie Tate, Jennifer Jenkins, Steven Rich, Keith L. Alexander, and Wesley Lowery, "Fatal Police Shootings in 2015 Approaching 400 Nationwide," *Washington Post*, May 30, 2015.

Big Dreams and Bold Steps Toward a Police-Free Future

1   Originally published at *Truthout* on September 16, 2015.

2   See http://fergusonaction.com/demands.

3   Ibid.

4   Organization for Black Struggle, "Quality Policing Initiative," available at http://obs-stl.org.

5   See www.joincampaignzero.org.

6   Graham Rayman, "Eterno and Silverman, Criminologists, Say NYPD's Crime Stat Manipulation a Factor in Recent Corruption Scandals," *Village Voice*, November 29, 2011, available at www.villagevoice.com.

7   Bernard E. Harcourt and Jens Ludwig, "Broken Windows: New Evidence from New York City and a Five-City Social Experiment," *University of Chicago Law Review* 73, no. 1 (Winter 2006): 271–320, available at http://lawreview.uchicago.edu.

8   According to Communities United for Police Reform. See http://changethenypd.org/issue.

9   "Cops or Soldiers?," *The Economist*, March 22, 2014.

10   See www.laforyouth.org.

11   See http://cangress.org/our-work/share-the-wealth.

12   See www.spirithouse-nc.org/collective-sun-ii.

13   See http://alp.org/community/sos.

14   The StoryTelling & Organizing Project (STOP) is a project of Creative Interventions, a resource center committed to creating and promoting community-based interventions to interpersonal violence: domestic or intimate-partner, sexual, and family violence. See www.stopviolenceeveryday.org.

15   Ending broken-windows policing is the first in a series of solutions proposed by Campaign ZERO. See www.joincampaignzero.org/brokenwindows.

We Charge Genocide

1   Originally published at *Truthout* on September 23, 2015.

2   Adam Hudson, "1 Black Man Is Killed Every 28 Hours by Police or Vigilantes: America Is Perpetually at War with Its Own People," *AlterNet*, May 28, 2013, available at www.alternet.org.

3   The name comes from a 1951 petition to the United Nations, which documented 153 racial killings and other human rights abuses, mostly by the police.

4   The video "For Damo" can be viewed online at www.truth-out.org/opinion/item/32911-we-charge-genocide-the-emergence-of-a-movement.

5   Mariame Kaba, "We Do This For Damo . . . ," *Prison Culture* (blog), May 20, 2015, available at www.usprisonculture.com.

6   Mariame Kaba, "To Damo, With Our Love . . . ," *Prison Culture* (blog), December 1, 2014, available at www.usprisonculture.com.

Heeding the Call

1   Originally published at *Truthout*, with original artwork by Sarah Rosenblatt, on March 7, 2015.

2   Mary Green, "Oprah Winfrey's Comments about Recent Protests and Ferguson Spark Controversy," *People*, January 3, 2015.

Our History and Our Dreams

1   Originally published at *Truthout* on September 22, 2015.

2   See Britney Schultz, "Taken from Families, Indigenous Children Face Extreme Rates of State Violence in US," *Truthout*, July 12, 2015.

3   "Stop Angela at Wounded Knee," *Chicago Tribune*, March 24, 1973.

4   Quintard Taylor, "From Esteban to Rodney King: Five Centuries of African American History in the West," in *The American West: The Reader*, edited by Walter T. K. Nugent and Martin Ridge (Bloomington, IN: Indiana University Press, 1999), 282.

5   William Loren Katz, "Africans and Indians: Only in America," William Loren Katz (personal website), February 23, 2007, available at http://williamlkatz.com.

6   For example, in the Crazy Snake Rebellion of 1909.

7   Derek Royden, "The Other 1%: Healing the Wounds of Native American Tragedies on Turtle Island," *Occupy.com*, September 2, 2015, available at www.occupy.com.

8   See Kelly Hayes, "Transformation, Reparations, and Radical Education," *Transformative Spaces* (blog), March 4, 2015, available at http://transformativespaces.org.

A New Year's Resolution

1   Originally published at *Truthout* on December 26, 2014.

2   Tongo Eisen-Martin, "We Charge Genocide Again! A Curriculum for *Operation Ghetto Storm: Report on the 2012 Extrajudicial Killings of 313 Black People by Police, Security Guards and Vigilantes*" (study guide published by the Malcolm X Grassroots Movement, May 2013), available online at http://mxgm.org.

3   Mike Ludwig, "'Walking While Woman' and the Fight to Stop Violent Policing of Gender Identity," *Truthout*, May 7, 2014.

4   American Civil Liberties Union, "The War on Marijuana in Black and White: Billions of Dollars Wasted on Racially Biased Arrests" (report published June 2013), available at www.aclu.org.

5   Ibid.

6   Mike Ludwig, "Why the People of Ferguson Can't Trust the Cops," *Truthout*, August 21, 2014.

7   Jihan Hafiz, "Special Report: Ferguson Police Profiling of Blacks a Major Funding Source for City Budget," *Real News Network*, October 3, 2014, available at http://therealnews.com.

8   FBI Uniform Crime Reports, "Crime in the United States 2012: Table 55," available at www.fbi.gov.

9   See www.drugwarfacts.org.

10 For example, the Harm Reduction Coalition, a national advocacy and capacity-building organization, works to promote the health and dignity of individuals and communities who are impacted by drug use. See http://harmreduction.org.

11 See Mike Ludwig, "While Congress Fails on Syringe Exchange Funding, Activism Fills the Gap," *Truthout*, December 21, 2014.

12 See Ching-In Chen, Jai Dulani, and Leah Lakshmi Piepzna-Samarasinha, eds., *The Revolution Starts at Home: Confronting Intimate Violence within Activist Communities* (Brooklyn, NY: South End Press, 2011).

Community Groups Work to Provide Emergency Medical Alternatives Separate From Police

1   Originally published at *Truthout* on September 14, 2015. Some original supporting documents referenced in this chapter are available to view online at http://www.truth-out.org/news/item/32782-community-groups-work-to-provide-emergency-medical-alternatives-separate-from-police.

2   See http://criticalresistance.org/chapters/cr-oakland/the-oakland-power-projects.

3   Critical Resistance, "Victory for Oakland Residents as City Attorney Dismisses Controversial Police Gang Injunctions," (press release, March 6, 2015), available at www.commondreams.org.

4   Critical Resistance, "The Oakland Power Projects" (report published March 2015), available at http://criticalresistance.org.
5   See http://whitebirdclinic.org/cahoots.

Building Community Safety

1   Originally published at *Truthout* on August 25, 2015.

Index

About Haymarket Books

Haymarket Books is a nonprofit, progressive book distributor and publisher, a project of the Center for Economic Research and Social Change. We believe that activists need to take ideas, history, and politics into the many struggles for social justice today. Learning the lessons of past victories, as well as defeats, can arm a new generation of fighters for a better world. As Karl Marx said, "The philosophers have merely interpreted the world; the point, however, is to change it."

We take inspiration and courage from our namesakes, the Haymarket Martyrs, who gave their lives fighting for a better world. Their 1886 struggle for the eight-hour day reminds workers around the world that ordinary people can organize and struggle for their own liberation.

For more information and to shop our complete catalog of titles, visit us online at www.haymarketbooks.org.

Also Available from Haymarket Books

Exoneree Diaries: The Fight for Innocence, Independence, and Identity
Alison Flowers

Freedom Is a Constant Struggle: Ferguson, Palestine, and the Foundations of a Movement
Angela Y. Davis, edited by Frank Barat, foreword by Cornel West

From #BlackLivesMatter to Black Liberation
Keeanga-Yamahtta Taylor

I Am Troy Davis
Jen Marlowe, Martina Davis-Correia, and Troy Anthony Davis, foreword by Sister Helen Prejean

How Capitalism Underdeveloped Black America: Problems in Race, Political Ecoomy, and Society
Manning Marable, foreword by Leith Mullings

9 781608 466122